Travels with a Princess

JAYNE FINCHER

TRAVELS WITH A
PRINCESS

A Decade of Photographing Royalty

Weidenfeld and Nicolson · London

To Alan

Text and photographs © Jayne Fincher, 1990

Published in Great Britain by
George Weidenfeld & Nicolson Limited
91 Clapham High Street
London SW4 7TA

Printed and bound in Great Britain by
Butler & Tanner Ltd, Frome and London

Page 2: the Princess of Wales in Abu Dhabi, 1989.

Contents

Introduction

It was a cold, damp February morning in New York. For several hours I had been standing on the same spot, pressed up against a police barrier, trying to hold on to a precious vantage point outside the seedy, neglected Harlem Hospital.

It had been pouring with rain, and I was in need of a hot drink. But Harlem is one of New York's most depressed and deprived areas, and I doubted whether it was safe for me to wander about looking for a coffee shop with expensive cameras dangling around my neck.

A Royal visitor was due on the scene, and already a massive security operation was under way, with sniffer dogs inspecting bins and bags, and burly policemen diverting pedestrians across the road.

The Princess of Wales was in New York for a three-day visit and wherever she went I was supposed to be. Her engagement at the children's AIDS unit at the hospital was one of the key events and the final appointment of her itinerary.

Eventually the cold and damp weakened my resolve, and I decided to change my position and settled myself into a spot inside the hospital foyer, where I perched myself atop a small step ladder which raised my head above the crowds.

Getting in and out of cars can often make a good photograph. The movement of a dress can make the picture look so much more glamorous than when a person is just standing in front of you.

Here we see the Princess of Wales arriving for a banquet held by the President of Nigeria at Claridge's Hotel. The Princess's gown is shown off to its best as she steps from her car.

As usual, it was one of those assignments that required me to wait for hours on my ladder to ensure a good clear view. It was well worth the wait for this nice fashion shot.

About ten minutes before the Princess was due to appear, a very aggressive television crew decided that they wanted to get a better position, and set about it regardless of who was in the way. A row broke out with some other press photographers and a scuffle developed. As I was perched immediately behind them, I soon found myself tumbling through the air from the top of my ladder.

A large FBI agent caught sight of the melée and, seeing me leaping about, assumed that I was at the root of the trouble and decided to throw me out.

After a lengthy explanation, and support from some of the royal visit organisers, I was allowed to stay. But despite all the effort it was hardly worth while because in the end I was unable to see the Princess through all the security men.

It is a rough-and-tumble world packed with battles against bureaucracy and the weather, demanding deadlines, punishing airline schedules and cultural taboos, all of which require more than a little help from Lady Luck. It is not made easier by the fact that I am a 31-year-old woman working in what is essentially a world dominated by men. Sometimes I wonder if I am totally mad to have chosen such a career. But after 13 years as a photographer I am wrapped up in it and cannot change.

It is a challenging and varied life with the chance of meeting kings and queens, princes and princesses, and presidents and prime ministers.

And the circumstances in which I meet them can change dramatically. For instance, the chaotic and dreary scene which I have described when trying to snatch a picture of the Princess of Wales at the Harlem hospital was a world away from the venue of only a month or two before. Then I was able to photograph the Prince and Princess of Wales and their two sons alone in the charmingly informal but private surroundings of Highgrove, the Gloucestershire house which is their country home.

No policemen. No FBI agents. No barriers. No

bureaucracy. it was on the occasion of the Prince's fortieth birthday. And I had them all to myself.

It is a job which can be terribly frustrating at times, especially when I despair of capturing the right picture in those fleeting moments. And yet it can be hysterically funny as well.

That little story from my 1989 diary is a typical example of the dangers, dilemmas and disappointments which are a routine part of the everyday life of a professional photographer working on the international circuit for newspapers and magazines.

The extensive travel programmes which the Royal Family undertakes every year have provided marvellous opportunities for me to visit places that most people could never hope to see – scenes brought to them only through still or TV cameras. And the opening of such exclusive doors has enabled me to photograph many notable and distinguished people.

A fascinating career and life style, one might say, but also a punishing daily schedule of hard work which demands endless patience and adaptability, as I hope to show you.

Often people ask whether I get bored with photographing the same subjects time and time again. I always answer no emphatically, and I mean it. It is a constant fascination to me that I am in a position to witness so many historical events and capture them on film for future generations to study. The British Royal Family remains very popular and is held in awe by so many people in this world of radical change.

In 1980 I was standing on yet another cold pavement. On that occasion I was outside London's Ritz Hotel to cover the arrival of guests for Princess

Margaret's fiftieth birthday party. Rumours were rife that Prince Charles' new girlfriend might be attending, but I had no idea of what she looked like.

A tall young lady, only a few years younger than myself, tried to squeeze through the small crowd of press photographers. We moved aside to let her pass through. Only a little later did we realise that we had all just missed the 'prize shot' – the arrival of Lady Diana, the girl we had all moved aside for.

That slip-up by the camera corps meant another very late night of waiting – waiting for the party to end. And that resulted in my first photograph of the future Princess of Wales – a woman who, in the ensuing ten years, I have photographed probably more than any other member of the Royal Family. And I am sure that I shall continue to do so for many years to come, perhaps even in her role as the Queen of England....

I have so many vivid memories of exciting events that have taken place during my travels.

One such event which I shall always remember was in Rome in 1985 when the Prince and Princess of Wales visited the Vatican for an audience with the Pope. I was one of a handful of press photographers allowed in to record this historic meeting.

After taking the pictures, we were very surprised when the Prince of Wales ushered the Pope over to us and introduced us. I was very nervous and turned a bright shade of red. I did not know just how one should greet a Pope – curtsey or kiss his hand? I tried to remember what the Princess of Wales had done but my mind went blank. Somehow in the end I muddled through.

Some of my most interesting foreign tours have been following the Princess Royal on her trips to Third World countries as President of the Save the Children Fund. These journeys have been such a contrast from the luxury of palaces and all the pomp and ceremony.

Princess Anne seems to have an endless supply of energy, and I have had great difficulty in keeping up with her fast pace with all my camera gear over my shoulders.

In late 1984 I travelled to India and Bangladesh to cover her visit there, a trip which I will never forget. Not only was it the first time I had ever witnessed such terrible poverty, but the tour also coincided with the tragic assassination of Prime Minister Indira Gandhi.

We were only a few days into the second week of the tour and had just arrived in India. The Princess was due to visit the hill town of Mussourie, nestling

This is one of my favourite studies of the Princess Royal, and I took the picture in northern Bangladesh during the Princess's tour in October 1984.

The Princess had been visiting projects connected with the Save the Children Fund in remote villages and was dressed very casually in jeans, a cool shirt and a sun hat over a headscarf.

I felt unbearably hot and looked absolutely exhausted as we arrived at a village school, but the Princess stood in the shade of a hut looking cool and neat as she chatted to teachers. I wondered just how she managed to look so good. I particularly like the Princess's expression – thoughtful and rather far-away.

in the Himalayan foothills, just a few hours' flying time from New Delhi.

It was during a tour of a school in Mussourie that we first heard of the shooting in New Delhi. But at this stage it was all rather sketchy. Princess Anne was whisked back to New Delhi on the Royal Flight but unfortunately there was not enough space for myself and two colleagues, so we had to borrow the British Embassy Range Rover, which the Princess had been using, to transport ourselves back to the capital.

When I reached New Delhi I was totally immersed in the task of covering the assassination, followed by the State funeral, and, alas, the rest of Princess Anne's tour was cancelled.

I spend much of my working life – can you believe it – standing on the top of a small set of portable, aluminium steps. This little ladder from Woolworths has travelled the world. It provides me with the vital extra height that can make all the difference in obtaining a clear view above the crowds of people, fellow photographers and tall policemen, and quite a few 'snappers', as we are known, use them.

Carrying this ladder provokes a great deal of comment, amusement and even incredulity. When crammed into a rush-hour train with my ladder, many businessmen look at me with raised eyebrows, obviously regarding me as either totally mad or a somewhat over-dressed window-cleaner. Airline staff are frequently quite miffed when some twenty passengers (my colleagues and me!) check in and board the plane with twenty ladders. We tell them that we are on a global window cleaners' convention.

My colleagues on the royal road are for the most part male. This means at times it can be quite lonely being a female in the press corps. I am sure my fellow photographers at times get a little confused as to how they should treat me – should they push me out of the way, as they do with each other, or be gentlemen?

Well, usually they just treat me as one of the lads and I have to stand my own ground, although sometimes I find this physically impossible. Even though I am no weakling I often prefer to crawl through their legs to reach the front, climb behind

them on to my ladder or, whilst they are all in a scrum, smile sweetly at a policeman or security official and slip into a position at the side.

I am pleased to say that there are at least a few female journalists who often travel with the 'Rat Pack'. This unsavoury description was bestowed by a local paper on the travelling press corps from London during a royal visit to Australia in 1983. The title has stuck.

I have travelled by all means of transportation while following the royals around the globe. In 1977 I travelled to Africa to cover the Queen's tour. As the Press group was relatively small it was decided that the best way to enable us to keep up with Her Majesty as she flew from country to country was to accompany her luggage on an RAF Hercules transporter plane. It was not the most comfortable way to travel among the crates of mineral water and suitcases.

In 1987 I greatly enjoyed the experience of flying in a sea-plane. We were to photograph the Duke and Duchess of York in a remote Canadian location as they departed by canoe for a private holiday. The

OPPOSITE
At the end of their official tour to Canada in July 1987, the Duke and Duchess of York planned a ten-day adventure holiday in the wilderness of the Canadian North-West Territories.

The Duke and Duchess agreed to pose for photographs at the 'splash off' point. We had been forewarned by locals to prepare ourselves against the blackflies that are prevalent in the tundra by wearing protective clothing and netted hats. We scoffed slightly at the warnings and thought they must be exaggerating.

We flew from Yellowknife on a fleet of small sea planes up to the Caribou narrows. As our planes came to a halt we could see the royal couple and the rest of their holiday party playing a game of frisbee and all wearing netted hats and protective jackets. As we stepped out of the planes we were horrified to be surrounded within seconds by swarms of blackflies – we should have taken the advice of those locals.

The Duke and Duchess were wonderful and removed their protective fly gear for our photographs. They sat very patiently on the edge of their canoe, trying to keep the flies away from their faces, without spoiling the photographs, by continually waving their hands about. Fortunately, you cannot see from the photographs just how uncomfortable it was having to endure those flies.

splash-off point was a tiny island, and the only way for us to reach it was by a fleet of these small planes chartered from Yellowknife. It was the first time I had ever flown in a sea-plane, and the flight was surprisingly smooth.

Remembering a flight in Thailand will always bring a smile to my face. The press had been flown by the Thai Air Force to spend the day in Chiang Mai. The outward-bound journey was uneventful, but on our return to the airstrip, in anticipation of boarding our flight, we were suddenly thrown into a panic. Our plane was sitting totally alone at the edge of the runway ... no lights, no sign of life. ... The reason we were so anxious to take off on time was that many of us were due to connect with a flight back to London from Bangkok.

We wandered around the aircraft trying to see if anyone was on board, and a few of the men decided to pull up the aircraft steps to take a closer look. By this time we all had the giggles and it was a funny sight when *Daily Express* photographer Steve Wood climbed the steps and started to bang on the doors, calling out, 'Let us in, is anybody there?'

Nobody answered, so we sat ourselves down on the runway and waited. We waved goodbye to the Prince and Princess of Wales' flight and still waited.

Sometime later a truck arrived with the aircrew, all looking rather well-fed and totally unmoved by all our rantings and ravings, who proceeded to unlock the plane. It appeared that supper had been a more important priority for them and the mad English Press corps just had to wait.

Over the years, I have had the chance to glimpse some of the most lavish interiors. During the Prince and Princess of Wales' visit to the Gulf in 1986 I was overwhelmed by the opulence of the Arabian palaces, and one of the most dazzling was that belonging to King Fahd of Saudi Arabia.

I could hardly walk across the rooms as my feet sank into the deepest hand-woven carpets I have ever seen, and I found myself being mesmerised by all the sparkling chandeliers and golden objects. To be allowed into this domain as a woman was virtually unheard of – the strict Moslem customs restrict access for women to such places. But on this tour the Princess and her household, plus myself and a few other female journalists, were given the honour of being allowed into places normally reserved only for men.

The King's palace was one of these areas, but we were only there for a short time while the Princess met the King, and were then escorted off to a

On the last day of our visit to Kuwait with the Prince and Princess of Wales in February 1989, I took one of my best photographs of the trip.

The Prince and Princess visited the Kuwait Museum, interesting it itself but not for photographs. However, outside in the museum courtyard there was the perfect setting. Colourful Bedouin tents had been set up, the floor was covered with brilliantly patterned carpets, and dancers and musicians had been brought in to entertain the guests as they drank coffee.

After the refreshments the Prince and Princess were presented with gifts, which included two Arab robes. The Princess looked on with delight as her hosts gently lifted the garment out of its box. It was very exotic, covered in gold sequins and beads. Her hosts gestured for her to try it on, and as usual she did not disappoint them.

Pandemonium broke out among the ranks of photographers on the opposite side to where I was standing. Fortunately I could see the Princess in her gown, but my colleagues could not as there were too many security men in the way.

Quickly I took my shots, before the mob descended, and, fortunately for me, by the time they all reached my position the Princess had just taken off the robe.

women's-only dinner at another palace. Prince Charles, meanwhile, stayed for dinner with the King.

I thought this was a good chance to gain access to photograph the Princess with some of the local princesses and, for a change, not to have to jostle with my male colleagues for a position.

Alas I was disappointed as custom reared its head again. The taking of photographs of Arab women is forbidden in Saudi Arabia.

During the Gulf tour I also enjoyed what must have been one of the most unusual press lunches ever. The Prince and Princess were invited to a desert picnic, again in Saudi Arabia, and as they sat down to lunch with their hosts in huge Bedouin tents we were escorted to our own tent.

The floor inside the tent was covered completely in Persian rugs, and a traditional Arab feast was served to us by men in colourful robes. A terrible thought crossed my mind; would I be presented with sheep's eyes to eat? Luckily roast lamb was on the menu, but I stuck to spicy rice.

Another unusual meal for me was in the Sudan in 1987. I was following the Princess Royal on her visit to a Save The Children camp in a remote area called Umballa. Our accommodation was in a large straw hut usually reserved for 'cholera' patients. Conditions, as one would expect, were very primitive, and we had been advised to bring from England some pre-packed food. I had loaded my bags with Marks and Spencer's lamb stew and dumplings.

After spending the day touring the camp and witnessing at first hand the horrendous effects of famine, I felt very guilty going back to our hut to cook my food on a campfire. As I sat eating out of a tin, I offered our local guard some of the stew. Despite the fact that food was not plentiful to him, he looked at the food rather fussily and was not at all impressed with the flavour when he scooped a mouthful. I always think of him whenever I am looking at the delicious products in Marks and Spencer's foodhall.

Taking the photographs is only a part of a day's work. As the saying goes in Fleet Street: 'You can have the best picture in the world, but it's no good if it's sitting in your camera bag.'

It seems to be a constant race to meet deadlines and catch flights with couriers. Unfortunately, when on overseas tours, we do not have the luxury of keeping all the exposed film together and carrying it home with us. The competition and varying deadlines for publication call for the films to be sent back to London on a daily basis. This is not as simple as it sounds, particularly with the current problems of drug smuggling and terrorism. A few years ago I often found it possible to hand the film to an obliging passenger who would carry it safely to London. Now, however, they look at me with deep suspicion or report me to a security guard.

Trying to compete with fellow photographers in beating deadlines can often cause scenes rather like those in a farce. After declaring to each other that we are dead tired and definitely not going to send films home that day, we are often later spotted sneaking out of the hotel – airport bound. On reaching the terminal we will often find our colleagues lurking behind pillars trying to dodge each other whilst waiting for a courier.

In the past I have had to carry a portable darkroom on overseas tours to enable me to 'wire' a photograph back to the London newspapers. This attracts a lot of curiosity among the hotel staff when they see the bottles of smelly chemicals lined up in the bathroom with processing tanks. And they cannot work out why you have locked yourself in the wardrobe, often the only light-proof place in which to set up an enlarger – not a recommended place to work, especially in a hot country. Luckily, in recent years, the technology has changed and it is no longer necessary to carry such equipment.

At the end of these tours I feel absolutely exhausted. It seems almost as if I have been on the go twenty-four hours a day for the whole visit, what with all those worries over camera positions, press passes and flights. On the first visit to Australia by the Prince and Princess of Wales in 1983 the press corp had over *forty* flights.

Each time I flop down in my aircraft seat I wonder how long I will continue to do this....

As you flick through the pictures in this book or, indeed, in a newspaper or magazine in the future and spot a royal photograph, spare a thought for the miles that we may have had to carry those lenses and ladders, or the hours of waiting for that fleeting split second of photography. I hope you enjoy the photographs as much as I enjoyed taking them.

The Queen visited several countries in Africa in 1979, and although during the visit we photographed her many times with various leaders and dignitaries, we had no chance to photograph her with ordinary local people. It was, therefore, a welcome scene when the Queen arrived in Lilongwe in Malawi.

An enormous crowd of local women surged forward to greet the Queen as she stepped off the plane. It was a sea of black arms and hands among brightly coloured dresses. They were all dressed identically in these ceremonial robes with a picture of Dr Banda imprinted on the front of each.

The contrast between the colourfully dressed women and the Queen in her formal dress and hat with long white gloves and handbag, served to illustrate the visit perfectly.

∽ 1 ∽

By day and by night

Princess Michael looks equally stylish in her country clothes and her extravagant gowns. Here at the Badminton Horse Trials, while watching the cross-country, she wears a Tyrolean-style hat over a headscarf.

These horse shows always absolutely exhaust me – it is a case of trudging miles around the cross-country course in the hope of bumping into a royal. Thank goodness, at Badminton the main attractions are usually fairly near the press tent and one can sit and wait to spot a royal Range Rover's route before marching off in the wrong direction.

When I am photographing Royal events and tours, choosing what to wear is a constant problem for me, whereas it is, I imagine, a much more straight-forward matter for the royal ladies when they flick through their diaries and wardrobes.

Being a female photographer has its disadvantages when it comes to dressing; feeling comfortable and yet being appropriately turned out do not always mix well. Can you imagine me balancing on the top of my ladder in a long dress, or sprinting for a position in the press pen in a skirt and heels?

Like many women I like to be nosey and study what other women are wearing, and I always find it particularly interesting to note just how the royal ladies are dressed. Many of my male colleagues consult me if they need a little help to describe the name or style of a garment for a picture caption.

I must admit to having the giggles at times when a male reporter will say, for instance, 'Jayne, have you seen that green dress the Princess is wearing before?' That 'green dress' usually turns out to be blue, and not a dress but a suit!

Evening events such as banquets and film premières are popular with the photographers because they give us a chance to picture the royal ladies at their most glamorous with swirls of taffeta and sparkling gems. Attending all these functions gives me a wonderful opportunity to observe them, rather like a fly on the wall, but often I feel rather out of place wearing my working clothes against a backdrop of all that finery. . . .

I do, however, try to dress as smartly as possible because I feel it would be a shame for a very elegant event to be marred by a rabble of photographers in the corner clad in jeans and sneakers.

On some occasions, especially foreign tours, a dress code may be laid down for the press corps, but the rules seem to have slackened and this occurs less frequently nowadays. The men may, however, be required to wear dinner suits, and the female photographers cocktail dresses.

It was necessary to pack a long dress for the Gulf Tour in 1986 when the press were required to dress appropriately for a dinner in Bahrain. I had to kneel in the front row of the photographers to find the right vantage point, but suddenly found myself pinned to the floor when I tried to move off quickly. Another photographer was standing, unwittingly, on the hem of my long dress! I had awful visions of losing my skirt as I tried to stand up, but was fortunately spared that embarrassment.

Usually I have a rule never to wear a skirt of any length when I have to work on my ladder, following an amusing experience I had while photographing the Princess of Wales in London.

I was mounted on the ladder by a hotel entrance, and the public crowds immediately behind us were pressing closer to get a view of the Princess. Just as she stepped from her car, someone put their hand up my skirt and pinched my bottom. I leapt into the air and yelled to my male colleagues that I had been assaulted. But they all fell about laughing and did nothing to try to catch the offender as he ran off. I saw the funny side of the incident and had to laugh – even though I missed all the pictures.

State banquets are invariably lavish affairs and provide excellent opportunities to photograph members of the Royal Family in exotic gowns and priceless heirlooms such as tiaras and diamond neck-laces. They also wear family orders and jewellery or insignia given perhaps by their hosts.

The banquets held at London's Guildhall during state visits are usually very formal affairs. Guests are seated in a large hall for a welcoming ceremony before processing into dinner, while we position our-selves on a minstrels gallery overlooking them all. We have to work very quietly, and often I have this dreadful feeling that I shall drop one of my camera

Princess Michael of Kent attended a 'fancy dress' ball at Osterley in Middlesex with her husband in 1985. The Princess looked wonderful in a very full blue gown covered with sparkling beads, and with long ostrich plumes fastened to her tiara. She towered above the other guests.

The Prince was not so confident in his appearance – he kept very discreetly out of the way of photographers.

I am pleased to say the photographers were not required to join in the 'dressing-up'.

In July 1989 the Duchess of York spent the day with the all-female crew of the yacht Maiden sailing off the Hampshire coast. The yacht was undergoing sea trials in preparation for its entry into the Whitbread Round the World Yacht Race.

It was one of those engagements when the Duchess would not be able to wear formal clothes. After seeing the crew all dressed in shorts and t-shirts, the ever optimistic press photographers kept their fingers crossed that the Duchess might be clad in the same gear. When she arrived at the quay-side we were a little disappointed to see her lovely legs covered up, but we were still happy to see that she was very casually dressed in a tracksuit.

OPPOSITE
An elegantly dressed Duchess of York arrives in Portsmouth for a naval dinner aboard Nelson's flagship HMS Victory.

It was a really windy evening, and as the Duchess stepped out of her car I was struggling to keep the camera still. The Duchess was also having a spot of bother with the weather, with her long gown flapping about madly, but luckily for me it seemed to blow the dress out and give the picture a little more movement.

I always feel totally under-dressed when I have to undertake an assignment at Covent Garden's Royal Opera House, where the Gala performances are always very glamorous occasions. I remember one particular performance by Joan Sutherland – for once, I was there to photograph a non-royal person. At the end of her performance, as the curtain went down, I had to creep on to the back of the stage in order to get some shots of the famous singer taking her final bow. I got rather carried away and somehow found myself at the front of the stage. I was just about to fall off the edge, when a stage-hand hanging about on the side lines kindly grabbed me before I tumbled. It was most embarrassing, as you can imagine, with the whole audience watching my little side show.

Here, however, no such event occurred as Princess Margaret arrived wearing a brilliant red gown and numerous sparkling diamonds. She is seen greeting fellow guests before taking her seat in the Royal Box.

lenses from the balcony and see it land on some prince or princess's head.

State banquets at Buckingham Palace are also very grand events, and give me the feeling that I am in an episode of *Upstairs Downstairs*.

The press corps is led through a maze of scrubbed corridors beneath the palace, passing underground kitchens and staff rooms before climbing many flights of stairs until, suddenly, we pass through a door and feel carpet underfoot. There we see, in one of the magnificent rooms of the Palace, the Queen and her guests surrounded by fabulous paintings, antiques and hordes of uniformed footmen.

The Queen usually favours smart dresses and matching coats for her official outings, and on her days off we often see her at a horse show or polo match dressed in a more casual twin set with a woollen skirt and, of course, the familiar headscarf.

The Princess Royal also loves to wear headscarves during her 'off-duty' hours, usually worn with jeans and sweaters. She also needs a casual wardrobe for her frequent visits to Save the Children projects in remote, underdeveloped countries, where it would be both inappropriate and far too hot to wear formal dress.

Usually the Princess chooses cool, cotton shirts, sunhats, jeans or lightweight trousers and sports shoes. Despite the heat of the day in some of these more extreme climates, one rarely sees Princess Anne looking even mildly sweaty or ruffled. It beats me just how she manages to remain so neat and trim. One glance at the press corps would reveal a hot and dusty gathering of individuals, sweating profusely and looking a real mess.

The Princess did have the benefit of a home-made shower when she stayed at a refugee camp in the Sudan, which was erected next door to her mud and straw hut.

Meanwhile, members of the press were accommodated in a large straw hut that was used as a cholera hospital during any outbreak of the disease. We were relieved to be informed that there were no patients in residence at the time, and that no cases had been reported for some weeks.

But it was necessary to treasure every single drop of water there. Before leaving the city to head out into the wilds, we had not been forewarned to arm ourselves with enough water for washing ourselves. Imagine, please, the colour of our skins when we returned to our city hotel. I shall never forget the shade of my bath water in Khartoum after our expedition upcountry.

*Princess Margaret stands in the elegant hallway of her
London home at Kensington Palace.*
   *The Princess stands in front of a famous painting by
the Italian artist Annigoni. It shows the Princess in her
younger days with a short hairstyle.*

The Queen in one of her most formal gowns, a heavy dark-green velvet cloak, processing into Edinburgh Cathedral to attend the hour-long service to install new knights to the Order of the Thistle.

These ceremonies are potentially marvellous for photographers but it can be very difficult if we are placed in awkward camera positions. Here we had a great problem in getting a clear shot of the Queen as she walked beneath a long awning at the front of the Cathedral. With scaffolding posts dotted along the edge of the red carpet it meant that we kept getting a pole across the picture. Luckily for us, however, some of the older dignitaries proceeding ahead of the Queen were walking rather slowly, and as they battled with the Cathedral steps the Queen had to stop momentarily to avoid catching up with them. Everything was just right as she stopped in front of us, and I was very pleased with my photograph.

The Queen rarely wears trousers and, in fact, apart from jodhpurs I have seen her wear them only once. She was visiting a game reserve in Zambia during her African tour, and she chose to wear a pair of straight trousers and a blouse.

The younger female generation of the Royal Family wear trousers frequently, mostly in their private lives but occasionally, if an official engagement requires special clothes, they are to be seen in a variety of overalls, trousers or tracksuits.

It is difficult to pick out the most elegant dresser among the royal ladies, all of whom have their own taste and style. Often I wonder whether they ever confer with each other about their planned choice of attire before attending an event. I have noticed on several occasions that there has been a dominant colour.

At the Easter Service at Windsor in 1989, the Queen, the Queen Mother and the Princess of Wales all wore shades of pink. At the Derby in 1988 the Queen and the Princess Royal both wore similar shades of yellow.

While some people may consider it trivial to dwell so much on the clothes worn by our royals, it is a subject which will continue to fascinate all royal watchers, and frequently many a royal outfit has been known to boost the British fashion industry.

OPPOSITE

The Ruler of the United Arab Emirates, Sheik Zayed bin Sultan, held a banquet in honour of the Queen during his state visit to London in July 1989. This formal event was held at Claridge's Hotel.

These events are always rather frustrating for photographers as we are restricted to taking photographs at various intervals and only when instructed, such as when guests arrive and when they formally line up in front of us. For the remainder of the time we watch all the members of the Royal family arriving and greeting each other affectionately with kisses and curtsies, but at this point we are not allowed to take photographs.

The Queen is seen here in all her state banquet regalia – the diamond encrusted tiara is one of a number of elaborate jewellery pieces she wears here. On her shoulder, pinned to silk bows, are her two personal family orders. Family orders are small cameo paintings of kings and queens of the British Royal Family. Those worn here show the Queen's father and grandfather.

RIGHT
The Duchess of Kent is a keen singer and belongs to a number of choral societies. Here she was as gracious as ever and spared a few seconds for the photographers when she arrived for a rehearsal in Kings Lynn.

The Duchess, one of the most elegant royal dressers, looks smart in both her day and evening clothes, and here she looks cool in a cotton dress with her famous blonde hair swept back.

LEFT
Dressed up in formal evening wear, the Duchess of Kent sits patiently through a speech when she was a guest at a banquet held by London's Lord Mayor. Her choice of gown looks rather 'bridal' – all white organza and lace.

I was positioned on a balcony above the Duchess, and with a little patience and a lot of holding of breath it was possible to get a good clear shot of the royal guests from this position, although it is always rather embarrassing when a lull in the speeches emphasises the whirr of motor-driven cameras above the royal heads.

I could not quite make out what the Duchess of Gloucester was wearing when she attended a banquet held in honour of King Fahd of Saudi Arabia in London back in 1987.

The Duchess's evening gown was covered up with a large shawl of white taffeta pinned at the front with a large diamond brooch, and she did not look particularly comfortable in this outfit with all her heavy jewels. I often wonder whether royal ladies end up with a bad headache after having to sit all evening wearing a tiara.

ABOVE
Visiting a charity project in Ash, Surrey, the Duchess of Gloucester smiles broadly after collecting an armful of posies from children. It is always a pleasant assignment to photograph the Danish-born Duchess who is very charming and always looks so fresh and happy.

In recent years the Duchess has become very fashionable in her choice of clothes. Back in the 1970s she always stuck to rather predictable classics but now she experiments with colours and designs, and it suits her well.

The Princess Royal was entertained to dinner by President Ershad during her visit to Bangladesh. During the tour the Princess was seen mostly dressed in jeans and very casual wear, but for dinner a little dressing up was required. She wore a four-strand pearl choker and a long evening gown, and stood out among the other female guests who were all wearing colourful saris.

OPPOSITE
Dressed all in black, the Princess of Wales stands elegantly during the Armistice Day ceremony in Paris in 1988. The black hat has a Garbo-style net which seems to emphasise her large blue eyes.
   Despite this being a nice study of the Princess, lacking the necessary colour it was not popular as a cover shot.

❧ 2 ❧

Privileged moments

P hotographers who cover the Royal Family's activities dream of having one of them pose exclusively for them alone. With no pushing or battling for a key position or pool pass, it sounds an easy assignment by comparison with the tension and tough competition of royal tours. No doubt it will surprise you when I tell you just how taxing this kind of assignment can be – especially on one's nerves!

I am extremely fortunate and privileged to have had a number of opportunities to take some special, exclusive pictures to mark a royal celebration or event. This kind of job usually begins with a surprise telephone call from a private secretary, discreetly asking whether you are available. From that moment onwards one starts both to plan and panic. (I wonder whether really famous photographers get as uptight as I do before such events? I am sure Lord Snowdon and Karsh of Ottowa do not sit biting their nails and feeling more than a little sick at the prospect.)

My first experience of an exclusive photographic session came during a visit to Norway in 1981. I was there to cover the visit of the Queen and Prince Philip, and during the tour the summons came. Ron

Bell of the Press Association and myself were asked to go on board the Royal Yacht *Britannia*, berthed in Oslo Harbour, to take some personal shots of Prince Philip. They were to be issued to newspapers and magazines to mark the Prince's sixtieth birthday.

It was a nerve-racking experience, but it stood me in good stead for future assignments of this type. I learned just how quickly and efficiently one needs to work for those few precious moments when a member of the Royal Family is sitting right there in front of you. One does not keep them hanging about! It also taught me that it really helps if one can try to form some sort of plan in one's mind about the kind of picture envisaged. Just looking around the room at the last minute for a location can waste valuable time.

On this occasion Ron and I had to think very quickly as we were guided into the drawing room of *Britannia*. As neither of us had any special photographic lights with us, our eyes instantly focused on a desk situated next to a small porthole through which the sun was shining. We quickly decided that if the Duke sat at the desk we would be able to use this natural light source. The Duke agreed and we took our shots before the sun disappeared behind a cloud. When looking at the pictures back in the office it was easy to be critical, and we wished we had had the chance to put a small light here or there to enhance the pictures. But, unfortunately, on that particular occasion we had not the luxury of time.

Of course, it is not always possible to plan the shot you want to take, but a little thought goes a long way. Such a plan was very useful in 1986 when my father, Terry – a fellow photographer – and I were asked jointly to take some pictures of the Duke and Duchess of Kent for issue on their Silver Wedding Anniversary.

We both went to St James's Palace in London beforehand to look at the location – a small, stone

---

This photograph of Prince Edward was taken in the grounds of Windsor Castle.

When looking for a spot to take the photographs I was instantly attracted by the colour of the stone and the shape of the door set into the wall. The Prince happily stood by the door and I manoeuvred myself to keep my reflection out of the glass window.

Just as I was about to take a shot I noticed in the corner of my eye something moving . . . was it the ghost of Windsor Castle? – no, it was a footman passing by whose reflection appeared very prominently in the window.

courtyard. It needed some careful thought to imagine just how we were to photograph the royal couple against this plain, stone scene, without any grass or flowers, and yet avoid having grey, colourless pictures.

We decided to try to bring in flowers, which always brighten weddings and special occasions, so we set out to get some white roses of York, which had made up the Duchess's original wedding bouquet. But I found that they were unobtainable at that time of the year, and so we compromised with a combination of delicate spring flowers. I had to nurture them in the car all the way from home to London, spraying them frequently with water to prevent them from drooping. We arranged them in a garden trug to look quite casual, as if the Duchess had just picked them from her garden.

I was rather worried as I balanced the trug on the Duchess's lap, quickly trying to wipe off any dirt because I dreaded making any mark on the beautiful cream skirt she was wearing.

The pictures turned out very well, with the sun breaking through the dull clouds just in time to highlight the Duchess's blonde locks. Pictures with and without the flowers were issued.

In 1987 I was asked to take the official pictures for the Grand Knockout Tournament being organised by Prince Edward to raise money for charity. Fleet Street became very angry at being excluded from the event, but it was decided that by keeping the pictures exclusive we were likely to raise more for charity.

To this day Fleet Street still refers disparagingly to the Knockout event, but what most newspapers conveniently forget (and have never published) is that Prince Edward and his teams of other royals, sports and showbiz personalities raised over £1 million for four very worthy charities.

OPPOSITE

I was very excited and honoured to have been chosen to take the pictures of the Prince of Wales for his fortieth birthday, and in July 1988 I drove down to Highgrove House for the appointment. I had racked my brain to try to think of how I could photograph the Prince differently from all the other official pictures.

As I walked round the beautiful garden I spotted a lovely shaped window surrounded by a twisted vine. I asked the Prince if he would mind sitting in the window with the family's little dog known as 'Tigger'. Tigger had been following us around and I am sure he did not want to miss out on getting in the picture.

The Prince seated himself in the window frame and must have thought I looked like a garden statue as I stood outside on my famous stepladder in order to raise myself level with the window.

Unfortunately, the ladder was gradually sinking into the soft earth, and I had to balance very carefully in order not to look completely stupid by falling off. This was a rather difficult exercise as at the same time I was trying to attract Tigger's attention and worry about the bad light exposure.

BELOW LEFT

The glamorous Queen Noor of Jordan shares a happy moment with her daughter Princess Inman in the sitting room at their summer palace in Aqaba.

I found the Queen a real pleasure to photograph with her model-like looks and wonderful smile. I felt extremely dowdy and short standing next to the tall elegant Queen.

BELOW RIGHT

King Hussein of Jordan poses with his daughter Princess Ayesha in the gardens of his summer palace in Aqaba.

It was a wonderful opportunity to be able to spend a few hours at the palace photographing the family. It made a change to see the King relaxing off duty as a family instead of seeing him on television talking about the problems of the Middle East or busy at some conference.

ABOVE

*Prince Philip photographed here in the main sitting
room aboard the Royal Yacht* Britannia. *The pictures
were taken for issue on his sixtieth birthday.*

*A table by one of the portholes provided a suitable
setting in which to photograph the Duke. This shot was
one of only about three exposures that I managed to
take. Luckily, despite terrible nerves, I had got them
sharp.*

OPPOSITE

*One of only a few shots taken of Princess Margaret as
part of a feature of Her Royal Highness at home.*

*In all the photographs she looked very lovely standing
in the subtle autumn sunshine in her garden at
Kensington Palace. The Princess had thoughtfully
dressed in a vivid blue silk dress, despite it being pretty
chilly and it stood out well against the natural colours
of the garden behind.*

The event was described as having been too
undignified to involve members of the Royal Family,
but at no time did I see any of the royals do anything
undignified, and everyone clearly had a great deal
of fun.

While the Knockout was very hard work, it was
a success. Months of planning took place to ensure
in advance that we would have enough photographs
for British and foreign newspapers and magazines
and also to fill two books. I was extremely impressed
by the capability of Prince Edward who proved
himself to be a first-class organiser and a very good
producer. No other professional could have done a
better job, I feel sure.

A totally different special assignment came with
the opportunity to photograph the Prince of Wales
for his fortieth birthday in 1988. I was surprised
and highly delighted to be chosen. But as the actual
day dawned for me to travel to Highgrove to take
the pictures, I felt like a lump of jelly with nerves.

I drove down to Tetbury, a town near Highgrove,
arriving there very early to avoid any unforeseen

delays, and decided to have a cup of tea to calm me down. That was not such a good idea – my hands were shaking so much that I ended up nearly spilling it all over my clothes.

But once I had arrived at the scene and got underway with the photographs I felt a lot better. The Prince and Princess were charming and put me at ease immediately. Both of them were by then very professional in the art of being photographed, and they stood patiently while I checked my light meters and re-loaded film.

It was a golden chance to meet the two young Princes, William and Harry, who were running about just like any other little boys, pestering their mother to be allowed to go out to play. But they sat very still for their photographs and smiled when they were told, although I think Prince William was becoming rather fed up with having to have his hair brushed. Boys will be boys, and young princes are no different.

In 1984 I had a very welcome assignment to photograph some non-British royals. I was in Jordan at the end of the tour by the Queen and Prince Philip when I found myself and a colleague reporter being granted a little time to interview and take pictures of King Hussein and Queen Noor.

That turned out to be a most memorable few hours which we all spent at their Aqaba Palace on the shores of the Red Sea. The King and Queen made us both feel very welcome and, after taking some shots of the Queen in her sitting room, the King suggested that we should all go into the garden to see their children. That was indeed a bonus for us. We had not expected to be allowed to see the Princes, let alone include them in photographs.

When we had finished taking our shots, we were invited to have coffee. And as we sat sipping it overlooking the Red Sea, I wondered what other job in the world would provide one with such a fascinating afternoon, with a privileged insight into the private lives of kings and queens.

Prince Edward is photographed here dressed in his costume as a team captain for the Grand Knockout Tournament held in 1987.

I had the pleasure of taking the exclusive still photographs of the event that was organised and directed by Prince Edward for charity. The event received strong criticism from Fleet Street and I think it was totally unfair. The papers were not given access to the event, and a bit of green-eyed jealousy started to creep in. Not once have I ever seen a report of how much good has been done with the funds raised. As a result all sorts of projects from many worthy charities such as the Save the Children Fund and the World Wildlife Fund have been undertaken.

The Duke and Duchess of Kent in one of the official photographs issued for the celebration of their Silver Wedding in the spring of 1986.

The picture is taken in a small courtyard at St James's Palace where the couple has an apartment.

Despite being quite an overcast day, the sun managed to shine through just at the right moment to create a soft, summery effect.

❦ 3 ❦

A day at the races

Generations of the Royal Family have had a passion for horse racing. The Queen and the Queen Mother seem to have been the most enthusiastic race-goers in recent years. Both own racehorses and the Queen has her own breeding stud.

The younger generation of royals seem to regard a day at the races a little more light-heartedly as a chance to meet friends and have some fun. But the Queen's love of horse racing has been passed on to two of her children, Prince Charles and the Princess Royal. With strong, adventurous natures, they were not satisfied to act merely as spectators – both wanted to be jockeys.

The Prince of Wales trained hard and rode in a number of races, including the Military Gold Cup at Sandown in 1981. The newly-engaged Lady Diana Spencer was there to watch the Prince race, along with his mother and grandmother. And they saw him fall at one of the fences and end up with a very bloody nose. He looked furious with himself for having fallen, and, perhaps, all the more for having done so in front of the family and his new fiancée.

I remember also having been furious with myself on the same day. I had been rushing around all over the place to take pictures, firstly of Lady Diana in the paddock, and then to find the right fence to position myself by during the race.

I chose what I thought appeared to be the most ominous challenge – and Prince Charles cleared it

beautifully! He galloped on, however, only to fall a few fences later.

When we realised that the Prince had fallen, my colleagues all rushed off to the other fence to see what had happened. But owing to a ski-ing accident on a previous royal tour, I had only just had my leg taken out of plaster, and I could barely walk, let alone run, across a racecourse. And so I had to give up and hobble back to the unsaddling enclosure.

Princess Anne has also ridden in a number of races at well-known courses like Sandown, Kempton Park and Worcester. The Princess Royal has to fit keep-fit training in between her official engagements. Like her brother she has had some falls, but luckily she has escaped injury and they have not deterred her.

The most prestigious British race meeting is, of course, Royal Ascot held in June each year. This is, in effect, a 'pilgrimage' for the Royal Family, members of high society and the fashion leaders, as well as the ordinary punters.

It is an event with which I have a love-hate relationship.

On a warm, sunny day it is delightful to stand on the press balcony and watch the endless parade of ladies in the latest fashions – especially the hats, for which Ascot is famous – or to watch the parades in the green paddock, or the traditional strawberry and champagne picnics.

But on a cold blustery day there is nothing worse than waiting for hours on end in the freezing wind until the royals arrive after lunch.

It is the old story about my work – the need to arrive everywhere long before the event starts in order to seize and defend a prime position for taking pictures, and this is never more important than on the balcony at Ascot.

Unfortunately the press are never allowed to take photos from ground level, and must stay on this first-floor balcony. This breeds chaos because we

Two royal Princesses mingle with the crowd in the Royal Enclosure at Ascot.

Sir Angus Ogilvy accompanies his wife, Princess Alexandra, and her cousin, Princess Margaret, down to the paddock.

Judging by their happy expressions, they must have backed a few winners!

share the area with the owners and trainers of race-horses, and it becomes very over-crowded.

But Ascot is a highly colourful occasion, steeped in tradition, and no-one can miss it. Members of the Royal Family arrive in a procession of horse-drawn landaus just after lunch. The scene is a sea of hats of all shapes, colours and sizes. The crowds of racegoers line up right along the route of the royal coaches, and applaud politely as the procession passes.

The only way to spot a member of the Royal Family among the thousands below the balcony is to keep your eyes peeled. My own trick for this is to

The racy ladies' hats usually capture all the attention of the photographers at Ascot. But it is hard to ignore the fine top hats worn by the Royal Prince and the Duke of Edinburgh with their morning coats. Here a dapper Duke is pictured at the Epsom Derby.

The Princess Royal appears confident as she prepares to mount her horse, Cnoc-Na-Cuille, for a race at Kempton Park in 1987.

She looked very professional in her colourful racing silks and jodhpurs. Although she was not placed, she rode well and did not come off – much to the disappointment of some of my colleagues!

try to memorise the colour or style of the hats that each one is wearing. Take your eyes away from the camera lens for just a second or so, and you can lose them for hours.

The Prince of Wales rarely seems keen to stay at Ascot for too long. When we see his car arrive at the back of the Royal Box, usually shortly after the first race, we know that he is about to slip away to play his favourite sport, polo. But the Princess of Wales and the Duchess of York rarely hurry away from Ascot. Both set the scene in the finest fashions, and they seem to enjoy popping down to the champagne bar in the paddock to link up with their friends. And guests of the Queen in the Royal Box usually include a number of carefully chosen friends of the Princess and the Duchess.

One of the best opportunities to photograph the Royal Family at Ascot is when they walk down through the Royal Enclosure to the paddock before a race – towards our camera position. But one snag here is that we are quite high up, and it can be very difficult to see their faces, especially as they usually wear large-brimmed hats for the occasion.

During the early years of Princess Diana's visits she presented us with quite a challenge to see just who could get a picture showing her face, because she always tried to avoid the cameras by walking shyly with her head down.

This habit caused a problem for one of the stewards at the Royal Enclosure gate, where there is always a very strict check on badges. The steward did not recognise Princess Diana and stopped her – then realised his mistake and looked most embarrassed.

You may find this hard to believe, but in all the years that I have attended Royal Ascot I have never once seen a race. The reason is simple. The press balcony is at the back of the Royal Grandstand,

Whilst the rest of the Royal Family were studying the racing form very seriously, the Princess of Wales had the giggles about something she had spotted. Princess Diana was standing alongside her sister-in-law, the Princess Royal, to watch the runners of the 1986 Derby canter past to the start. The Princess Royal, unaware of the Princess's giggles, looks very serious as she tries to pick a winner.

and as my photographic 'spot' must be guarded jealously, it is impossible to leave it to watch a race.

This makes life very tedious, and so we pass the time watching the world go by, looking at the fashions, and usually making critical comments about the hats we see. But the strict code of dress at Ascot requires me also to wear a hat, and this drives me crazy because it is very difficult to take a photograph with a hat on your head.

I have been lectured a number of times for removing it briefly to take a picture. Now I tip it backwards in a ridiculous style to ensure that I can get the camera to my eye, before shoving it forwards again. The milliner who designs my hats would die if he saw the manner in which I have to wear his creations.

Derby Day is not such a formal event in the racing calendar, and fortunately for me the dress code is not as strict. The event is held on Epsom Downs and, while still a royal occasion, it is a world apart from Ascot.

It is a day out for the public, and is always crowded

A proud grandmother is accompanied through the crowds in the Royal Enclosure by the Prince of Wales during Ascot week.

Racing etiquette at Ascot demands that when members of the Royal Family walk down to the paddock, a pathway is kept clear for them to walk back to their Royal Box. Fellow racegoers traditionally line the edge of the pathway to applaud the royal party on these occasions, and I am able to get a closer glimpse and pictures.

The winner of the fashion stakes at Ascot nowadays is invariably the Princess of Wales.

In 1988 she wore her own version of a top coat in grey silk. I was lucky to be able to catch this picture of the Princess in the unsaddling enclosure as she turned briefly and glanced over her shoulder. The breeze caught her coat just at the right moment and gave me this elegant fashion shot.

OPPOSITE
In a sea of hats, the Princess of Wales stands out as she moves through the paddock at Ascot in 1989. She wore a very large-brimmed hat designed by Philip Somerville, which was easy to spot from our highpoint, and we could see her face quite easily despite the slanting brim.

with day-trippers, with double-decker buses parked along the course as 'mini-grandstands' for their passengers. While the champagne and strawberries are abundant in the members' enclosure, Derby Day is much more of a hotdog, burger or fish and chips affair.

But I rarely enjoy covering the Derby because it always seems so cold, probably because our press post is on a high stand opposite the finish and seems to be the most exposed point on the Downs. Inevitably, it means an early start. We have to be at the course by about 8.00 am to establish a front-row place on the stand, and then it is a long dreary wait until 3.30 pm for the start of the great race – very boring hours.

The younger Royals are rarely seen at this famous racing event, although in recent years both the Princess of Wales and the Duchess of York have attended. But the Queen and Queen Mother both study racing form very seriously as the runners canter past them.

During the race we do not often see members of the Royal Family on their balcony until the last few minutes. They watch the start and the first half on television in the Royal Box. Then as the horses gallop up the final few furlongs of the course, the royals come outside to watch the finish, and we have but a few brief moments to seize our chance to take pictures.

But a day at the races can be a golden opportunity to take some pleasing off-beat photographs of royalty, relaxing far away from the endless handshaking rituals. And personally I like covering the races because it is a chance to capture good fashion pictures – although I usually drive back home with a bad headache after hours of scanning the dense crowds for a glimpse of a Royal hat.

ABOVE
*Sarah Ferguson was given a rousing welcome when she
attended Ascot races in 1986 only weeks before her
wedding.*

*Although the future Duchess had been a guest of the
Queen at Ascot in previous years this was the first time
she rode prominently in a carriage with the Queen
Mother.*

Two very serious racegoers watching the runners of the 1988 Derby at Epsom as they move off to the start of the race.

It has been the routine in recent years for the Queen and her party to gain a close view of the horses from the edge of the course as they pass by. In this picture the Queen looks a little worried at her choice, but the Queen Mother looks quite confident, perhaps in spotting the winner.

LEFT
The Queen Mother likes nothing better than a day at the races. Here she looks very relaxed when she attended the Military Gold Cup at Sandown.

⟿ 4 ⟿

And the wait goes on

If you added up all my time spent out on royal assignments over the year you would be surprised to see just what a large proportion of that time is spent not taking photographs but just waiting. Endless hours sitting on my ladder or pacing up and down a pavement – this is the side of my job that requires extreme patience.

I now equip myself with a few essential items: a good book, a raincoat, comfortable shoes, a mobile phone, and lots of change for parking meters. And with these necessities I find I can encamp myself quite comfortably on any pavement in preparation for a long wait.

The birth of a royal baby and the subsequent departure of the mother and infant from hospital can be counted among some of my longest waits.

Great excitement and panic builds up as the pregnant Princess or Duchess is admitted into hospital. We leap into our cars and head for the hospital to stake claim to a spot on the pavement, usually opposite the entrance.

A lesson was learnt by some of my colleagues in 1988 when they prematurely decided to pre-position their ladders outside the London hospital to which the Duchess of York was due to be admitted. They padlocked a number of pairs of steps to various lampposts and barriers. They were horrified to find the next day that their ladders had disappeared.

OPPOSITE

After missing the departure from St Mary's Hospital of Prince William, I was determined not to miss the Princess of Wales leaving with her second son, Prince Harry.

The Princess looked so glamorous despite only having had the baby less than twenty-four hours previously. We could hardly glimpse the tiny face of the little Prince wrapped tightly in a blanket.

ABOVE

Not quite so much press coverage for this new royal baby's departure from hospital but we still had a fair wait, and it was worth it to capture this gentle moment between mother and baby.

Princess Michael of Kent looks fondly at her new daughter, Lady Gabriella, as she left St Mary's Hospital in Paddington. The Princess's son, Lord Frederick, is anxious not to be left out!

The mystery unravelled as they discovered that the police had arrived equipped with metal cutters and a large van, and had taken the ladders away because they were considered an obstruction. It proved a nuisance to the owners of the ladders who had to go to the Police station to claim their property, and also to the police who had to complete the paperwork.

It provided us with a lot of laughter, however, during the monotonous hours of waiting over the next day.

One of my biggest photographic disappointments was in 1982 when the Princess of Wales had her first son, Prince William. I arrived at St Mary's Hospital in Paddington shortly after the Princess had been admitted. I grabbed a good spot in the press pen but found I would need a larger pair of steps. A small ironmonger's store around the corner couldn't believe their business for ladders in those few hours; they were completely wiped out of their stock of six-foot ladders. Once I had put my shiny new ladder in place I settled down happily to await the announcement that the baby had been born.

A very enterprising sandwich bar began a relay of sandwiches and teas between our press pen and their shop, keeping us well fed without the worry of having to leave our spots. I even remember sitting on my ladder eating strawberries and cream. We had every luxury except a loo on site....

The birth of Prince William was eventually, announced and we photographed the comings and goings of Prince Charles and other royal guests.

By mid-afternoon the following day I decided to go home for a rest, confident that the Princess could not possibly be leaving the hospital so soon after the birth. There was, as I vaguely recall, some sort of a train strike and as I drove through Hyde Park heading out of London the traffic was awful.

I switched on the radio and nearly had a heart attack when I heard the announcement that the Princess of Wales would be leaving hospital with the new baby within the next half hour. Panic set in as I swung my car around in the middle of the road, heading back to Paddington.

It was useless, I sat getting more and more frustrated in the traffic as it moved inch by painful inch. My heart sank as I felt I really was going to miss the Princess. I tried to park my car and run, but a vigilant policeman would not let me stop. I dodged in and out of the traffic and ended up bumping into the back of a taxi. I was desperate.

Eventually I neared the corner of the hospital but

A very exciting day, the wedding of the Prince and Princess of Wales in July 1981.

I was positioned in a building looking down on to the steps of St Paul's. It proved to be a good vantage point for an overall shot, but a little too far for close-ups. Here we see the bride and groom descending the steps to their carriage after the ceremony.

as I turned the corner I could see the royal cars just pulling off. My colleagues were meandering back along the street with huge smiles on their faces as they rewound their films.

Words failed me. I got out of the car and just burst into tears.

Luckily I have not repeated this performance in recent years and have managed to photograph *all* the departures of subsequent royal babies.

In 1988 we had a lot of fun waiting for the Duchess of York to leave the Portland Hospital with baby Bee. It is a very difficult street in a busy area of London's West End. A constant stream of office workers and shoppers makes it difficult to keep the press area clear. The biggest problem is parking, and early every morning we raced to London to beat each other to the meters.

One very funny incident took place in the final hours before the Duchess was due to leave. We had been allowed to park in one of the streets behind the hospital which had been sealed off by the police. Many of my friends had done this and there seemed to be no problem for a quick exit.

One colleague went off to his car and came running back very breathless and panicking because many of the cars had been clamped. Well, you can imagine the uproar, especially as many people had to dash off immediately with their films to meet deadlines. Those of us not clamped roared with laughter, but the others were, at this stage, in a fit of frenzy.

A police officer in charge was called over and the poor man met a heated barrage of complaints. Eventually he radioed the clamp unit and asked them to come down immediately and release the cars.

The Duchess calmly departed with her baby unaware of all the fuss only ten minutes previously. Thankfully we had our pictures at last and could now go home for a well deserved rest.

Royal romances and weddings also require many hours of waiting to get the perfect picture. When the rumours of a romance between Lady Diana Spencer and Prince Charles became more credible, and it was turning into a legitimate news story, I spent some time sitting outside Lady Diana's London flat waiting for a glimpse of, perhaps, a future princess.

It was winter and very cold so to keep warm the press would often gather in cars with the heaters on full blast. The trouble with this was that it made you fall asleep. On several occasions we all awoke from

ABOVE
The Duchess of York proudly shows off her new baby daughter, Princess Beatrice, as she leaves the Portland Hospital in London in 1988.

This was the result of many hours of waiting but these happy pictures prove it was all worthwhile.

OPPOSITE
A fleeting few minutes to capture the happy bride and groom as they emerge from Westminster Abbey after their marriage.

Some of us had stuck a large message on the front of the press stand, asking the couple to look over in our direction. I am not sure if they saw it but they certainly smiled at us.

One of the most colourful scenes of pomp and ceremony during the year is Trooping the Colour to celebrate the Queen's official birthday. The Queen is followed by a sea of red uniforms of Guards' officers on horseback as they process down the Mall in London.

It must be a tourist's dream to be present at this ceremony. It does not matter how many times I have seen this parade it still makes me feel very proud to be British.

a short doze to find Lady Diana had walked straight past us and driven off in her car.

It is always such a relief when the Palace finally announces to the world an engagement. When Sarah Ferguson was reported to be the future bride of Prince Andrew she found a large group of press outside her London office every morning.

We photographed Sarah arriving for work, and sometimes we hung around in the appropriately named 'Royal' coffee bar opposite to wait for her lunch break. Sarah was extremely good-natured with us, and even though we must have been awful pests she never once lost her temper.

At last at 11.00 am on 19 February 1986 the announcement came – they were engaged. I was lucky enough to be one of the small group of pool photographers allowed in to take photographs of Prince Andrew and Sarah in the grounds of Buckingham Palace. It was so nice to be able to take some good clear photographs instead of all the snatched shots of the past weeks.

The Royal Wedding approached and after months of letter writing and keeping one's fingers crossed, I was issued with a pass for the press stand opposite Westminster Abbey.

About a week before the wedding I decided to drive past the location to see if the stand was completed. I was horrified to see that not only was it ready but some of my colleagues had already chained their ladders and tripods into place.

I called the office and asked them to send up my gear immediately, plus a large marking pen. The pen was very important as already people had drawn out their exact spot on which to stand, and had left warning messages such as 'Do not remove – this is reserved'. I chose what I considered to be a good angle and proceeded to mark out my territory. For nights before the wedding I tossed and turned, hoping that no-one had removed my possessions or had taken my spot.

The wedding day dawned and I was on the stand in the early hours, relieved to find that no-one had taken my place. I spent hours before the service fiddling with my lenses and changing my mind every few minutes as to what to do.

After all that worry the pictures were just fine, I arrived home that night absolutely exhausted.

The wedding was over, but what about the honeymoon? Of course, these are private but sometimes the Palace grants us a facility at the beginning or end of a honeymoon to take some pictures of the newlyweds.

Romance was in the air for Prince Andrew and his new fiancée, Sarah Ferguson, when they posed at Buckingham Palace on the day of the announcement of their engagement back in 1986.

Here they are seen gazing fondly at each other as they stand on the steps of the terrace at the back of the Palace. Despite being a miserable grey day, nothing could dampen the newly-engaged couple's spirits. They laughed and joked around and eventually, after a lot of encouragement from the press, they quickly kissed.

The Prince and Princess of Wales were to cruise from Gibraltar down to Egypt aboard the Royal Yacht *Britannia*. I flew to Egypt with a number of colleagues and drove up to Port Said to photograph the yacht entering the Suez Canal.

There was much speculation as to where the royal couple would disembark, and I thought it a good bet that they would take a short visit to see the Pyramids and Sphinx at Giza on the outskirts of Cairo. After all, who visits Egypt and doesn't go to see the Pyramids? I had always dreamed of visiting this location, but I can tell you the novelty gradually wore off after sitting in the hot sun for a number of days, waiting to see if any of the important looking cars might be bringing royal tourists.

They never came, and we flew back to London very disappointed.

It was not long, however, before we cheered up. An informal photocall had been arranged with the Prince and Princess on their return to Scotland, and we all got our photographs.

Day-to-day royal appointments can also be quite time consuming. Film premières can often prove to be a great waste of time. For an 8.00 royal arrival it is often necessary to place one's ladder in position by 3.00. If you leave it later you end up in the third or fourth row and will have no pictures to show for it. However, these première arrivals do sometimes make very glamorous pictures, and unfortunately should not be missed.

The most unpopular assignment of the year for me is to photograph the Royal Family on Christmas Day attending the family church service. Normally this takes place at Windsor Castle but in the past few years it has been held at Sandringham due to renovation work at Windsor.

This job disrupts family life totally for me at Christmas, and the only compensation is that I can skive out of cooking the lunch! But the reason I grin and bear it is that it is one of the few opportunities that we have to photograph all the Royal Family together.

After a long drive to Norfolk, we take our places outside the church to photograph the arrival of the family. It can be very miserable having to stand in the cold or rain on Christmas Day waiting for the Royals to leave the church. To occupy those waiting hours I think of all my un-opened presents to rush home to . . . and the turkey cooking.

What is one more hour after a busy royal year of taking photographs?

A perfect romantic setting for a honeymoon photocall. The Prince and Princess of Wales on the banks of the River Dee which flows through the Queen's Scottish estate, Balmoral.

After weeks of trying to get some pictures of the Royal couple on their honeymoon in Eqypt, and having not succeeded, it was lovely at last to have a chance to photograph them.

5

Mums and dads –
sons and daughters

A t the end of a busy day of public engagements members of the Royal Family can go
home to put on their other hats as mums
and dads or sons and daughters. Private family time
is precious; busy official schedules and foreign tours
put many demands on family life.

I am sure a great deal of planning is undertaken
to ensure that especially the younger members of
the family have enough time with their parents. As
we approach the 1990s life has become a lot less
restrictive within royal circles. The children attend
normal schools in preference to being tutored at
home, and they have a lot more freedom to pursue
normal childish activities and mix with other children.

During the year we see just how important family
life is to our royals. Big get-togethers on such special
occasions as Trooping the Colour or seasonal holidays at Windsor, Sandringham or Balmoral provide
time for the family to enjoy a little privacy together
away from public duty. Christmas always seems to
be a jolly affair for the royals. Imagine the size of the
table as they sit down for Christmas lunch – there
must be at least twenty-eight adults and over ten
children. This is one picture I would love to have.

A complete family photograph is impossible to
take. The nearest we obtain is the scene on the
balcony of Buckingham Palace for Trooping the

*Despite being a dark December afternoon I am happy to
say that the pictures of Princess Beatrice's christening
turned out well.*

*The royal cars were held back for a few minutes before
collecting their special passengers to enable us to have
a clear view of the happy proceedings at Chapel Royal
St James's Palace in London.*

*Prince William, at only one month old, flew to Scotland
for his first Highland holiday at Balmoral in September
1982.*

*Despite the fact that I could not see the little Prince,
I was still pleased to be able to photograph the Prince
of Wales in his new role as a father. The moses basket
was gently carried down the steps of the royal aircraft
by the Prince as they arrived at Aberdeen airport.*

ABOVE LEFT
A happy family photograph of the Duke and Duchess of Gloucester with their three children.

The occasion was the christening of their newest daughter, Lady Rose, at the village church in Barnwell, Northamptonshire.

ABOVE RIGHT
A family wedding – Lord Frederick Windsor arrives with his mother, Princess Michael of Kent, for the wedding of his cousin, James Ogilvy.

Little Freddie giggled at the large group of press outside the door and he hurriedly scampered off after his mother.

The three heirs to the British throne sit together in the garden at Highgrove House.

I took this picture as part of a set of pictures for the Prince of Wales' fortieth birthday in 1988. The boys looked so grown up in their matching shorts and ties as they stood proudly next to their father.

Colour. The picture is never complete because a few members of the family are always missing.

Although we have the chance of photographing nearly every member of the Royal Family on Christmas Day it is not possible to get them together in one frame. We photograph them arriving and departing separately.

Another picture that is quite hard to acquire is that of The Queen and Prince Charles on their own. I had not realised this until a magazine asked for such pictures shortly before the Prince's fortieth birthday. As I searched through all my transparencies I noted that I only had the two together on two occasions.

It is easier to be able to photograph The Queen and Queen Mother together, especially during the racing season when they attend a number of meetings.

Another great opportunity to photograph the Queen with her mother is outside Clarence House on the Queen Mother's birthday. The family accompanies the Queen Mother out on to the street outside her home to receive flowers and cards.

Three generations of royal racegoers at the 1988 Epsom Derby. I particularly like this photograph because the serious expression on Princess Anne's face contrasts well with the natural and happy smiles of the Queen and the Queen Mother.

OPPOSITE

Photographers always get excited at the prospect of taking a picture of a royal baby, and one such event was in August 1989.

The Royal Yacht Britannia was due to set sail from Portsmouth for Scotland with the Queen, the Duke and Duchess of York, and baby Princess Beatrice on board.

I had missed, along with many of my colleagues, the chance to photograph Princess Bee some weeks earlier and I urgently needed to up-date my files as I had so far only photographs of the little Princess at her christening.

I was anxious not to miss this opportunity, and was worried that the press would not be given access to the quayside. To complicate matters, the Queen Mother's eighty-ninth birthday was the same day and this meant going to Clarence House in London to photograph the traditional scene of the Queen Mother in the street greeting well-wishers.

I planned my strategy with military precision. I could take the Clarence House photographs, then if everything ran to time I could just about get down to Portsmouth.

I decided to use two ladders for this busy day and sent one down with a colleague to Portsmouth earlier in the day to stake claim to a precious spot on the quayside.

As soon as the Queen Mother walked back to her home, it was one mad rush. To an outsider it must have seemed like the start of a Grand Prix as photographers and reporters screeched off to get to Portsmouth.

We need not have worried, for there was plenty of room and everybody was delighted with the happy pictures that we were able to take of Princess Beatrice.

This is one of my favourite royal photographs that I have taken, probably because it is so informal but also because it was a nice change to see the Princess 'off duty' with her sons, just like any ordinary young mother.

Here, sitting on the garden wall at Highgrove, the little group giggles as they glance in the direction of Prince Charles, who was standing alongside me. I shall not tell you what he was doing to make them laugh – that would be giving away one of my royal secrets.

When the Queen Mother celebrated her eighty-fifth birthday a special service was held at Sandringham church. It was lovely to see the Queen Mother being totally spoilt by her two daughters as she left the church. In the covered porch the Queen and Princess Margaret fussed around her, helping her on with her coat and acting as ladies-in-waiting with her flowers and presents from well-wishers.

I always think how strange it looks when I see the Queen's family greet her on formal occasions. At a recent banquet I was surprised to see them curtsey or bow before kissing their mother or aunt.

I have also noticed how the Queen's family refers to her as 'The Queen' when talking in public and that they never refer to her as 'mother' or 'my mum'.

It must be a hard task to be a royal mother especially when foreign tours mean separation from the children.

Shortly after the Princess of Wales had Prince William she had a six-week tour to Australia and New Zealand on her schedule. The thought of leaving her lovely new son was just too painful and

Trooping the Colour is always a day for a happy Royal Family gathering. The Queen's official birthday parade causes great excitement, especially among the royal children.

A chance to watch endless rows of marching Guards or ride in an open-topped carriage provides a fun day especially for Prince William and Prince Harry. The highlight for the children comes just before lunch as the family gathers on the balcony of Buckingham Palace with the Queen to watch a fly-past by the RAF. The two little Princes, along with many of their cousins, jump up and down excitedly, saluting their grandmother and pointing out certain soldiers who catch their attention.

In this picture, taken in June 1989, we see the Queen, Princess Margaret, The Princess of Wales and her two sons all looking up towards the sky, awaiting the arrival of the planes.

The Princess of Wales and her sons, Prince William and Prince Harry, arrive at Aberdeen Airport for a late summer break in Scotland.

People sometimes think I am mad to travel all the way to Scotland for just a fleeting few seconds of photography, but I think the journey is well worthwhile for the chance of taking some family photographs.

We do not often see the Princess of Wales with her mother, Mrs Shand Kydd, in public, so it was therefore a welcome opportunity to photograph them together at a family wedding in September 1989.

As the two ladies stand elegantly side by side in the door of the church it is clear to see from whom the Princess gets her height and svelte figure.

the Princess broke with tradition and took the baby on the tour with her.

Of course Prince William did not appear in public at all her appointments but to the delight of our press corps a photocall was arranged in New Zealand. It was to be held in the grounds of Government House in Auckland and we were very excited at the prospect.

We arrived early to ensure that a large rug on which we had been told the Prince and Princess would sit was in the right place. We must have moved that rug a hundred times before we all finally agreed it was in an ideal spot.

The pictures were super – the Prince and Princess casually sitting with Prince William playing in front of them. I wonder what the Prince thought of all this attention and so many people. He certainly was not shy as he showed us his newly learnt skills of crawling.

Another unwritten tradition that the Wales family seems to have dispensed with is that of not travelling together on the same planes, especially those in closest succession to the throne.

In 1982 the Prince of Wales arrived aboard the Queen's Flight in Aberdeen. It was a surprise to us to see the Prince descend the aircraft steps carrying a moses basket with Prince William lying in it. This was the beginning of a change of royal travel plans and over recent years we have seen the Wales family fly together on many occasions.

The sight of Prince Charles carrying that cot was wonderful. It was the first time we had really taken a picture of the Prince in his new role as a father.

The Princess Royal is one of the hardest working members of the Royal Family, and yet over the years we have had many opportunities to photograph the Princess with her children. She has worked hard to keep the children's lives as normal as possible; they do not even have titled names, they are plain Miss Zara and Master Peter Phillips.

Peter and Zara are obviously very close to their royal grandparents. They often spend the weekends at Windsor Castle and are frequently seen at horse shows or polo during an outing with the Queen.

One family holiday that usually begins around the end of August is the cruise on the Royal Yacht *Britannia*. The yacht slowly cruises from South-ampton up the western coast of the British Isles and finally drops its passengers in Aberdeen. It is usually only the Queen's closest members of the family who set sail on these voyages as accommodation is limited.

This must be a wonderful opportunity for the family to relax and just enjoy each other's company. During the voyage the yacht often anchors off a small island or near a beach to allow the royals to go ashore to take a walk or have a picnic.

The press of course try to speculate as to where the yacht will stop in anticipation of a good photo-graph but it is extremely hard to tail a yacht at sea.

The Royal Family continues to grow, and not since the days of Queen Victoria has there been quite so much young blood. As a new decade begins the Queen can look forward to the birth of her sixth grandchild.

Eight-year-old Zara Phillips was the newest recruit to the ranks of the royal racegoers at the Ascot race meeting in June 1989.

Zara joined her mother, the Princess Royal, a very keen jockey, in the Royal Enclosure despite the fact that the racecourse rules usually only allow children over fourteen. The Queen, however, owns the racecourse, so it was not difficult to obtain special permission for Zara's special outing.

Zara was on her best behaviour and was very proud of her smart floral dress and straw hat.

6

Far-away places

In May 1986 I travelled to Japan to cover the visit of the Prince and Princess of Wales.

I think I must have been jinxed, for I started the trip off badly. I had planned to go to Canada to photograph the royal couple's visit immediately before Japan, but only hours before my departure I learned a very hard lesson about looking after one's passport. Now I keep my passport safe at all times.

I had mislaid my passport, and after spending the entire night turning my office and home up-side down I tearfully called off the Canadian visit.

After very complicated re-arrangements of flight schedules, I flew directly to the Japanese city of Kyoto where one of the first fixtures for the Prince and Princess was a traditional tea ceremony.

Thank goodness I had not missed this event as it was there that we photographed the Princess wearing a kimono. It had been presented to Her Royal Highness after the taking of tea. The press, of course, were hoping she would try on the kimono, and we were delighted when the Princess obliged. It looked very funny worn over a western dress, and it clashed madly with the Princess's large red hat. It was also very large and swamped the Princess despite her height. With her usual good sense of fun she giggled at the long sleeves and tried to do a little shuffle to show off the garment to her delighted hosts.

It was later reported that the kimono cost over £15,000, a staggering amount, but, now knowing how expensive a place Japan is, I can quite believe it.

D uring the Royal Family's extensive foreign travels one of my main tasks as a photographer is to try to capture clearly in a picture something of the country or region which the Royal person is visiting without the reader having first to scan the story for details.

It is often a hard task to take a picture with an instantly recognisable landmark or background. Of

course such locations do exist, such as the Sydney Opera House, Red Square in Moscow or the Berlin Wall, and it makes life easier for us photographers if we can show a royal standing in front of a famous sight which needs no caption. But these photographs are not always plain sailing as it is often difficult to clear the background of streams of tourists, or diplomatically request the host or dignitary accompanying the royal visitor to stand aside for a clear shot. It must at times be a little embarrassing for a royal to stand there against a famous backdrop while his or her host is asked to step aside.

It does not always have to be a famous building to give a good picture a 'foreign flavour'; it could, perhaps, be an indigenous mode of transport such as a gondola in Venice or a camel in the Arabian desert.

Foreign dress can also be an added bonus to a picture. Although members of the Royal Family do not travel in foreign dress when they visit a country, there are often occasions when they are presented with gifts such as a kimono or a hat, and if they decide to try on the clothing then this often results in amusing photographs with that essential foreign flavour.

Australia has received many royal visitors in the past decade, and although it is a wonderful country it is one place that can be difficult to identify in a photograph. The cities often look very similar to those in Europe and America, and when a member of the Royal Family is visiting a hospital or art gallery, a photograph can end up looking much the same as one of an engagement in London.

The Prince and Princess of Wales visited Australia in 1983 and, during their long tour, part of their itinerary was to visit the outback. One of the most obvious images of Australia's outback is the kangaroo and we would have been delighted to have been able to photograph the Prince and Princess standing in a remote dusty location surrounded by these

The Duke and Duchess of York enjoyed an afternoon cowboy-style when they visited Medicine Hat in Canada in July 1986.

The Duchess was already wearing clothes with a Western theme – cowgirl boots and a suede fringed jacket – but the Duke was dressed rather formally in a lounge suit and tie. The Royal couple must have felt slightly out of place in the sea of stetson hats worn by their hosts and fellow spectators. Fortunately they were soon presented with matching stetsons to wear, much to their delight. They both burst into fits of laughter as they tried the hats on for size.

OPPOSITE
Royal tours always include countless airport scenes and we seem to be forever photographing members of the Royal Family stepping on and off a plane.

In February 1988 the Prince and Princess arrived in Bangkok on an official visit to Thailand. We found ourselves again waiting on the tarmac for the Royal guests. When they arrived, the Prince was guided off to inspect a guard of honour and the Princess was hidden by a sea of officials. It was beginning to look as though we were to get only a very ordinary picture of the royal couple walking along a red carpet and getting into their car.

Suddenly, some large colourful ceremonial umbrellas appeared, and to our delight we suddenly realised we might get a more interesting photograph after all.

The Princess was shielded from the hot sun by these umbrellas as she walked towards her car. This provided us with a chance of taking a photograph that at least had a little of the atmosphere of Thailand instead of being just another airport.

ABOVE
The Prince and Princess of Wales visited the Arabian Gulf in November 1987 and their first port of call was to the Oman as guests of Sultan Qaboos.

The Prince and Princess visited the modern university near the capital city of Muscat, and after touring the complex they were given a chance to spend time meeting students. It had not occurred to us that this occasion would provide us with an opportunity to show the differences in culture between Eastern and Western women. As the Prince and Princess approached the grassy area for the informal meeting, the Princess was directed off to the right to a group of female students and the Prince to his left to the male domain.

Much speculation had preceded this Arabian Tour concerning the Princess's choice of clothes in relation to local custom. The contrast of the Princess, with her short hair and bare neck, was excellent against the traditionally clothed young Omani ladies as they sat chatting and laughing together.

ABOVE
Just like other sightseers, the Duke and Duchess of York like to take photographs. Here they are both seen armed with their cameras when they visited Niagara Falls during their visit to Canada in 1987.

Our problem had been to clear the vista point of other tourists and dignitaries, but eventually we managed to get good clear shots with the royal couple in front of the Falls.

Venice, 1985, was hardly a romantic gondola ride for the Prince and Princess, pursued by a large number of Italian and British press.

The Prince looked a little worried as we picked our way precariously along the canal bank to follow them, but the Princess seemed to enjoy the chaotic scene. The ride was very short – only about 200 yards – but I think everyone involved would agree it was just about enough. Surprisingly, no-one fell into the murky water.

strange beasts, but this hope was just our imagination running away with us. We were lucky, however, for a chance to photograph the royal couple against the dramatic setting of Ayers Rock just as the sun set and the mystical landscape turned red.

Tours to such regions as the Gulf, the Far East and Africa can provide some magnificent settings for photographs. The Arabian Gulf, one of my favourite areas, holds much fascination for me. I enjoy photographing the elegant sheiks in their colourful flowing robes, especially when they are greeting visitors in the traditional manner, and I particularly like to cover the small but still important ceremonies such as the taking of coffee.

Another area that I love is Africa. Here, too, the local people are wonderful. During the visit of the Princess Royal to the Sudan in 1986 we visited some remote area in which The Save The Children Fund had been working very hard. I found it impossible to take in the scene of thousands of the camp inhabitants among the dusty mud huts on this barren landscape. It was a very difficult task also to show

67

The Princess Royal visited the Sudan in December 1986 to undertake one of her gruelling trips to some of the remote locations of the Save the Children camps.

One such place, Safawa, was large and overcrowded. Despite their extreme poverty and famine conditions the people were so friendly and gave the Princess a great welcome. They put on a small play with the help of camp workers to entertain their royal guest.

There was no pomp or ceremony and the Princess seated herself on an old box in the shade of a straw hut. It was difficult to show the scene as the actors were some distance from where the Princess sat. However, during the performance some faces of local women appeared in a cut-out window of the straw hut. This made a far more interesting picture than the Princess just sitting there on her own.

OPPOSITE

A highlight of the Prince and Princess's visit to Italy in April 1985, was their audience with the Pope.

As one of a small number of photographers allowed in to record the event, I felt very nervous, particularly as my male colleagues had been nagging me all morning as to what pictures I should take for them as the 'pool photographer'. (A pool means a situation where only a small number of photographers are allowed in to take pictures on the understanding that he or she shares them with the rest.) I could just imagine what they would say if I made a bad job of it – 'typical woman photographer....'

I arrived in rather a flap as I had not planned on being one of the fortunate few for this occasion and had not packed any appropriate black clothing, the customary requirement for a papal audience. I made do with a navy dress but still felt out of place as I walked along the splendid corridors of the Vatican heading for the salon where the audience would take place.

There was a hushed atmosphere, rather like that in a hospital where everyone tries to walk on tip-toe and speak in hushed voices. As I looked up it was rather like witnessing a biblical vision – the ceilings were elaborately painted with the most marvellous scenes.

The Prince and Princess arrived and entered the salon ahead of us for their private introduction. A small bell rang a few moments later to indicate to officials that the press should proceed into the room to commence taking photographs. The Pope stood with the Prince and Princess on a rug, at the far end of the room, patiently enduring our barrage of blinding flashes.

Once the photographs had been taken, Prince Charles introduced his household to the Pope and then, much

to our surprise, guided him over to our press corps for introductions. It put us all into a bit of a fluster, and as I filed out of the room a few minutes later I was still busy thinking about shaking the Pope's hand.

Suddenly I glanced down at my flashes and was horrified ... they were switched to the 'off' position. My heart sank as I suddenly thought I had totally messed up everything and the pictures would all be too dark. As I climbed on to the press bus I could not begin to think how to explain my mistakes to my other colleagues who were anxiously waiting to share these pool pictures.

My films were immediately flown back to London and I decided to go to my hotel room and quietly await the bad news from the colour laboratory in London. I could not face my colleagues in the bar downstairs until I knew the worst.

It was hours before I received a call from London – they were pleased with the pictures and everything was fine. I breathed a deep sigh of relief. Thankfully, I must have switched off the flash without realising it after all the excitement of meeting the Pope – or perhaps someone somewhere had performed a little miracle!

the Princess amidst all this activity in a few simple pictures.

I have been to Venice twice, firstly in 1985 for the Prince and Princess of Wales's visit, and secondly in 1989 for the Duke and Duchess of York's brief stay there. On both occasions the press wanted the obvious picture – a gondola bearing royal passengers. For the Prince and Princess this was to be, and a short journey was arranged for them one Sunday morning. We were excited at the prospect of what appeared to be quite an easy picture to take, and which would sum up this royal visit to Venice. We found out later that this was not quite so easy as it sounded.

Just prior to the royal couple embarking on the gondola trip, we repeatedly reminded the gondolier to ensure that he proceeded up the canal at only a snail's pace, to make it easier for us to keep up on foot. However, once he had his royal passengers on board, he seemed to find superhuman strength. He went so fast it almost appeared that he was driving a motorboat. Along the narrow canal the scene was chaotic as a large number of press, onlookers and officials all tried to keep up with the royal gondolier. The pathway at the edge of the canal was very narrow and everyone was trying to squeeze along with cameras, stepladders and television equipment.

One thing that none of us had noticed until we saw the processed film was a large ornate golden

Prince Edward visited Russia for the first time in April 1989. The short trip was based on his role as Patron of the National Youth Theatre which was in Moscow to perform Murder in the Cathedral.

Despite a busy rehearsal schedule the company had arranged for a quick sight-seeing trip to Red Square and the Prince was to join them.

Every visitor in Moscow has their picture taken in Red Square against the setting of the Kremlin and the colourful St Basil's. Our small press corps knew exactly what sort of picture we would like to take of the Prince – standing alone in a Russian-style hat in the Square. This was not quite as it turned out. The entire theatre cast turned up to have their photograph taken with their Patron which, I suppose, was fair enough as it was the reason for his Russian visit.

Next came the idea of persuading the Prince to wear a Cossack hat, one which had been purchased by a member of the press corps and was now in the hands of the Prince's private secretary with a request from us to him to wear. He obligingly did so, but unfortunately

because of the number of people milling about, and one or two of our press corps breaking ranks, it became impossible to get a good clear shot of the hat-clad Prince in front of St Basil's.

OPPOSITE
King Hussein and Queen Noor acted personally as guides to the Queen and Prince Philip during their visit to Jordan in 1984.

The royal party spent a morning viewing the spectacular 2,000-year-old 'Red Rose' city of Petra. Carved in the rocks, it is one of Jordan's unique archaeological centres.

Petra was sealed off to the public on this occasion, which allowed the British royal couple to wander around on foot at will or drive around the site in the Jordanian King's Range Rover.

In this picture we see the visitors standing in front of the Treasury – one of Petra's most famous buildings. It was a difficult picture to take because the group looked so small against the vast backdrop.

The Princess Royal visited some of the Arabian Gulf States in February 1987. During her short visit to Qatar the Princess was invited to ride some of the Amir's finest camels.

The date and time were set and I hurriedly arranged to scrounge a lift with a local photographer to the remote location in the desert on the outskirts of Doha.

Being the only two photographers, it was with great anticipation of getting a good photograph that we stood in the parched desert scanning the horizon for the Princess on a camel. Time passed and no royal rider appeared. Eventually a hot-looking British diplomat appeared from the distance to inform us that a rather embarrassing situation had arisen; the camels had not arrived. The disappointed Princess, after a long wait, had given up and gone back to the cool air-conditioned hotel. And I, too, was somewhat depressed as I had set my heart on this camel picture.

I had intended to travel on to Kuwait later that day but I heard that the Princess was keen to re-schedule her camel ride. I stayed in Doha awaiting news of the new location and time. The news came and again it was to a hot dusty spot that we travelled. Much to my delight and, I am sure, the Princess's, as we arrived we saw plenty of camels saddled up and waiting to go.

Again the local photographer and myself were directed to a suitable spot on the Princess's route, and there we waited. It was a very hot desert scene and must have been a rather bizarre sight for the Princess as she appeared over the horizon on her camel – two lonely photographers standing in the middle of nowhere waiting for her.

At last we had our photographs and the Princess had her promised ride.

bar that protruded from the side of the gondola on Prince Charles' side. In nearly all the pictures it appeared to stick up his nose or across his face. It was just one of those things that could not be helped and we just had to try to pick the clearest shots. At least we had the Prince and Princess in a gondola – unlike the Duke and Duchess of York who decided to stick to a motorboat for their entire visit.

During the Queen's visit to Jordan in 1984 the itinerary included two visits to historical locations, one to the Dead Sea and the other to Petra, the city carved in the rock. Although the visit to the Dead Sea was fascinating, we could hardly expect the Queen to put on a swimsuit and float in the salty waters. Instead, the Queen and the Duke stood on the banks with King Hussein and Queen Noor. It was hard to tell a story with the picture.

Petra, however, proved to be better pictorially. Despite the incredible size of the place, we were able to get a clear shot of the royal sightseers in front of the famous Treasury.

On some foreign tours the tranquility and atmosphere of a location can be totally spoilt by the noisy rumblings of a large press party accompanying the royal visitors. One such visit was to the Sultan's Palace in Yogyakarta in Central Java, Indonesia, in 1989. The press corps arrived about an hour before the Prince and Princess of Wales and it gave me a chance to wander through the Palace, which seemed to be made up of a number of open-sided buildings sited around dusty courtyards.

Leaving the hot sunlit courtyards and stepping up on to the marble floor of the palace rooms, I instantly felt the coolness of the exotic surroundings and could sense Indonesia's colourful and mystical past. Elaborate carvings adorned the Palace, and exquisitely dressed dancers prepared for a royal performance.

The Sultan and his wife, looking splendid in luxurious silk clothes, patiently stood at the Palace entrance awaiting their special guests. Outside, the

strangest guard of honour that I have ever seen lined the road. The men looked like real life-sized garden gnomes dressed from head to toe in red uniforms with tall pointed hats.

As the Prince and Princess's car drew up, the peace inside the Palace was suddenly shattered by the sound of dozens of pairs of step ladders being dragged across the floors and of the footsteps of over fifty press people jostling to be ahead of the royal party.

A few minutes previously, some horses adorned with colourful braidings had been standing quietly, but as the press charged across the courtyard the mounted guards had to struggle to hang on to their reins as the horses shied and panicked before peace was eventually restored.

I cannot begin to describe to you how hot it was during this visit to the Palace. It was not so much the sun but the unbearable humidity. It was the first time that I had ever really seen the Princess look uncomfortable, and as she sat watching the dancing

The Princess of Wales towers above two colourful ladies dressed in traditional costume from the island of Sumatra in Indonesia.

The Princess was visiting the theme park Tamrin Mini in Jakarta. Our press group persuaded the girls to stand in a prominent point at the exit so that we could try to get a shot with them in the same frame as the Princess to show the contrast between their styles of dress.

display she was clearly seen to say, 'I am so hot,' as she tried to cool her face down by blowing up towards her fringe. However, if you think the Princess looked hot you should have seen the colour of my face; never has it resembled a beetroot more than on this occasion. To make it worse we were all dying for a drink, and as we looked over to where the Prince and Princess were sitting we could see them being served with cool glasses of iced orange juice. Our tongues were virtually hanging out and we would have paid anything for a thirst-quenching cold drink.

The trouble with these tours in hot climates is that you move from one extreme temperature to another – hot and sticky one minute and the next absolutely freezing in an over air-conditioned hotel. It is no wonder that we usually all come home with colds.

Of course I just love it when Buckingham Palace announces a forthcoming visit for a member of the Royal Family to some exotic location, but often I regret that we have such a very short time to look around on our own. Often it is a case of arriving just before the royal guest, taking the pictures then dashing back to the press bus or airport to move on to yet another location. But I suppose it is better to have seen all these places for a few fleeting moments than never at all. . . .

In 1988 The Prince and Princess of Wales visited Australia to attend the Bicentennial celebrations, and it was half way through this visit when the royal couple attended a 'Surf Carnival' on the outskirts of Sydney.

We had conjured up visions of a typical Australian beach scene with the world famous bronzed hunky lifeguards. We were not to be disappointed. As we arrived ahead of the Royal party, teams of scantily clad lifeguards assembled for the prize-giving by the Princess. It was just what we photographers wanted, but suddenly uproar broke out when the lifeguards started to put on tracksuits over their swimming trunks.

This would spoil the pictures – we needed them to look exactly like bronzed Aussie beachboys. After a lot of cajoling they were finally persuaded to dispose of the tracksuits – much to the disappointment of the sponsors.

The Prince and Princess were sitting only yards away at this stage but seemed to keep their sense of humour during all these capers. The Princess giggled and turned a shade of pink as she stood among the lifeguards for a photograph with the award winners.

OPPOSITE

The Princess of Wales wears colourful garlands presented by the Nepalese girls during a visit to HMS Tamar *in Hong Kong. The girls were relatives of Gurkha soldiers stationed at Tamar.*

The Princess giggled at the garlands as she moved among the families during an informal walkabout.

☞ 7 ☜

Royalty in the rain

I am never quite certain whether it is the press corps or the Royal Family who seem to have 'rain-making' powers during official visits at home and abroad. On countless occasions we have spent a pleasant sunny day awaiting a royal arrival only to be soaked by a sudden, mysterious downpour that starts the very minute the royal visitor has stepped out of the car, train or plane.

In 1983 the Prince and Princess of Wales commenced their long tour of Australia and New Zealand from the outback town of Alice Springs, a sun-baked spot known for its lack of rain. The press arrived there twenty-four hours ahead of the royal flight, and we had visions of stepping off the plane to face a hot and dusty landscape. But we were astonished to find that there had been torrential rain and flash floods in the area for the first time in many years.

As we drove from the airport into town, passing swollen waters that previously had been cracked, dry river beds, we realised that the rain-making jinx had arrived ahead of us. We had spells of bad weather throughout the visit, especially in New Zealand.

I recall one engagement in Auckland where everything seemed to be going wrong because of the rain. The royal couple arrived and had to make their way carefully down a steep, muddy river bank to view

some canoes. The Princess, in a pale-lemon dress and light-coloured tights, was beginning to look a little mud-splattered, but managed to keep dry by wrapping a raincoat around her shoulders. We were absolutely drenched, and our cameras were so steamed up that it was virtually impossible to work.

Once the Prince and Princess had regained the comfort of their car, they were somewhat taken aback when it refused to start. An embarrassed chauffeur tried desperately to get the engine to fire, but had no luck because it was too damp. The royal couple had to continue their journey in one of the security cars.

To describe that morning's visit as a washout would be an understatement.

In 1984 the couple flew off for an official visit to Abu Dhabi – the last place one would expect to encounter rain. But, sure enough, the moment the aircraft doors opened and the royal visitors emerged, the rain started.

Neither carried an umbrella, which made it easier for us to take pictures. But it was not until we looked at the processed film that we noticed that the raindrops had marked the Princess's light-pink jacket, making it look as if she had spilt something down it. This was upsetting because the pictures were good, and it can be very difficult for a magazine to erase such marks for reproduction.

Why is it that I never seem to have a good raincoat or umbrella handy at the right time? Unfortunately the task of carrying all my heavy camera equipment, plus a ladder, rarely encourages me to burden myself with wet-weather clothing as well. Frequently I end up like a drowned rat and have a chill for weeks.

I always feel especially depressed if it rains when we are at some exotic, far-flung location. When the Duke and Duchess of York visited the tropical island of Mauritius in the Indian Ocean in 1987, I had expected nothing but clear blue skies. But we still had quite a lot of rain and grey clouds. One expects

The Princess glances up at the rain clouds as if to ask, 'Where is my umbrella?'.

Although well dressed for bad weather in a coat and hat, during her visit to Ardveenish on the Western Isles in 1985, she seemed a little fed up – everyone else around, including the Prince of Wales, seemed to have a brolly handy.

I have never seen the Queen looking quite so soaked as she was on this ceremonial occasion outside the gates of Buckingham Palace in June 1982. The Duke of Edinburgh and Prince Charles remained stiffly upright sitting behind her, while she huddled into her jacket as if to fend off the rain.

This was one of those days when I had left my own raincoat at home. I remember being soaked to the skin, but my priority on arriving home was not to change but to wipe off my cameras and put them in the airing cupboard to dry.

that sort of weather in Scotland, but not in Mauritius. I felt fed up, and I am sure the Duchess felt the same as we all looked apprehensively at the dark skies above.

The practical demands of working in the rain mean that the most important things to keep dry are the cameras, and not oneself. Once cameras get wet the electronics start to go wrong and the lenses mist up.

The wedding of the Princess of Wales's brother, Viscount Althorp, took place in September 1989 on a day that could not have been darker and damper. Heavy rain came down continuously as I tried desperately to keep my equipment dry by huddling under a little 'camp' of umbrellas that I had arranged.

But the trouble was that as soon as the guests started to arrive, I had to start taking pictures. I held my breath as much as possible to try to stop the back of the camera misting up, but it could not be avoided. All I could see through the viewfinder was a blur. This is the kind of occasion when one thanks heaven for new technology. I switched my camera to autofocus, and just pointed it in the right direction – and prayed!

I was delighted with the results. The shots were sharper than I could have obtained by focusing manually through the misted window.

Umbrellas in other people's hands can pose a problem for photographers. If the royal subject is huddled under a big black brolly, then we find it virtually impossible to get a picture of their face. But if the brolly happens to be held at a right angle, it can enhance the picture.

The Queen Mother is ideal for us because she usually carries a see-through plastic umbrella. It looks great in pictures. We can see her face quite clearly, and she keeps dry.

I can never decide which is the lesser of two evils for us photographers – the rain or the snow. While snow makes everything look so attractive, on the other hand it presents us with numerous problems and I have witnessed some hilarious scenes with my colleagues in the snow.

In 1984, the Prince and Princess of Wales agreed to a photocall in Vaduz at the start of their ski-ing holiday in Liechtenstein. A mass of photographers and reporters arrived at the chosen location, right next to the ski-lift, and my journey up the mountain with them had given me the giggles. It had been snowing heavily overnight, and the twisted mountain roads were covered with snow and ice. Only the

cars fitted with snow chains seemed able to cope with the conditions. Luckily the car in which I was travelling had them, but as the long procession of press cars climbed slowly upwards other cars dropped out and became stuck in the snow. We were cruel, laughing smugly as we overtook the opposition and left them behind.

On reaching the mountain top, we all scuttled back and forth around the chair-lift. As the royal couple started to move off, many of us scampered to different positions for a better shot.

What we did not realise as we moved about in the snow was that there was a deep drift under the lift, and suddenly we found ourselves waist deep and sinking fast. It was extremely funny as we all struggled to get out, striving desperately to keep our cameras up in the air and away from the snow. One photographer emerged with a long lens covered with snow and looking something like a king-size ice-cream.

It is also inadvisable to use a ladder in snow – as I learnt to my cost several years back at the Swiss ski resort of Klosters. I found my ladder sinking into the snow at a vital moment of the photo-call, and fell off, of course. Later in the car park I realised that I had also dropped my best exposed films from my pocket during the fall, and these must have been trodden down into the snow in the pandemonium.

I think that the coldest I have ever felt was during the winter of 1986 – one of Europe's coldest winters on record. I had travelled to St Moritz to photograph Prince and Princess Michael of Kent attending a British Ski Club of Great Britain event. The royal couple were due to watch a slalom race at the top of the mountain. It felt like the coldest place on earth as I stood awaiting their arrival. And I did not recognise them at first as they were so well-wrapped up against the extreme weather, with only their eyes visible. The Princess realised our problem and kindly

LEFT
Who is the mystery lady wrapped up against the weather during one of this century's worst winters? None other than Princess Michael of Kent.

And this royal lady knew full well how to keep out the cold with layers of clothing when she attended a Ski Club of Great Britain slalom in the Swiss resort of St Moritz. She kindly removed her scarves later so that we could picture her face, but personally I preferred to photograph her with that air of mystery.

Two royal sisters-in-law pose for the cameras on the slopes of Klosters in Switzerland in 1988.

Both were comfortably warm in their all-in-one suits and gloves, seemingly quite unaware of the fact that we photographers were freezing cold, nearly turning to snowmen, and standing about waiting for so long without being able to wear gloves to use our cameras.

I could barely wait for the photocall to end so that I could rush down the mountain and switch the car heater on.

ABOVE

The Queen Mother, ever thoughtful about her well-wishers, carries a see-through umbrella when she meets school children in Oslo in May 1982.

The rain did not deter her from visiting the British Embassy to meet the crowds, and the umbrella allowed both them and the photographers a clear view of this remarkable royal lady, despite the rain.

LEFT

The Duke and Duchess, however, were ill-prepared for the bad weather during their visit to Inverness in Scotland in 1989.

It was a very cold wet day, and by the time the royal couple reached their last walkabout, they were looking very damp. But they huddled under one umbrella, pulling faces and laughing with the crowd.

The Princess Royal looked very glum indeed as she stood in the rain at the Windsor Horse Trials in 1987. But, as an outdoor person, she was obviously well prepared for bad weather, with a full-length waxed coat and matching hat.

The Queen never seems to look so happy as when we picture her in a downpour of rain, she seems to absolutely love it.

Here in Kylesku in Scotland the Queen gives one of her radiant smiles while she stands under an umbrella as the rain continues to lash down.

took off her scarf and balaclava for a few minutes so that we could take some clear shots.

It was so cold that even my eyelashes were frozen stiff, and trying to touch the cameras was like putting my hand inside an ice box. Cameras just do not work properly in intense cold. The films become brittle and snap, and the metal casing starts to stick to one's face, which is so painful.

Back to the rain – and one person who really enjoys it. I have never seen the Queen happier than when she is in the rain.

However, I do remember one occasion when even Her Majesty seemed to despair of the weather, and

that was Trooping the Colour in 1981. I have never known rain to be so heavy. It seemed to become even worse as the Queen sat astride her horse outside the gates of Buckingham Palace. She hunched her shoulders and grimaced as her beautiful uniform became a soggy mess.

But despite my moaning about the weather, I have to admit that often these adverse conditions can add atmosphere to a photograph. It would be pretty boring if all the pictures were taken on bright, sunny days, even if it did make the life of a photographer a little bit easier.

8

The future generation

Lady Rose Windsor, the youngest daughter of the Duke and Duchess of Gloucester, is seen here looking very well behaved during an outing to Hyde Park in London.

A few minutes later however the little girl began to get a little bored with the official hand shakings and started to fidget and protest.

A nanny was quietly despatched with Lady Rose in tow.

I t is often said in the photographic world that the two worst subjects to photograph are animals and children.

I am happy to say, however, that having a growing number of royal children to photograph over the years has always been great fun. It is nice to observe that although these children are born into a way of life that many of us cannot comprehend, they remain in many ways just like normal boys and girls.

The centre of the future generation is, of course, Prince William, who will one day ascend to the British throne. This little Prince will always remain under the brightest spotlight, closely followed by his smaller brother, Harry. Both children are very charming but appear to have very different characters. Prince William seems to be a robust adventurous little boy, with an out-going nature, while Prince Harry seems shy and a lot quieter.

Both boys attended Mrs Mynor's kindergarten school in London before moving on to the Wetherby School. Press attention needs to be carefully controlled with regard to their school days. It could be very unsettling for the young Princes if they found a posse of photographers on the school steps every morning. A sensible solution has been to allow the press to be present on special days such as the first day of a new term, or the school Christmas play. This keeps the press coverage to a minimum and does not disturb the children too much.

I wonder if Prince William or Prince Harry have ever wonderd why we only call out their names as they arrive at school with their chums, or why they have to stand with their mother at the top of the school steps for a photograph.

The children seem to cope with all of this, they are very well-behaved boys and extremely polite. I was amazed a while back to see Prince William step off a royal flight in Aberdeen and stop to shake the airport manager's hand in a very grown-up manner.

Peter Phillips seems to be taking after his parents when it comes to riding horses.

The young man looked very confident on his pony as he cantered from fence to fence collecting results for the Windsor Horse Trials.

Peter dresses smartly in his pony club uniform complete with the club tie.

On some occasions, however, the 'little boy' instinct cannot be controlled, and once Prince Harry, arriving for school, could not resist sticking his tongue out at photographers.

It is not often that we see the young children of the Royal family attend formal official occasions; usually they only appear at such events as Trooping the Colour or family weddings. Of these special outings the children are very smartly dressed, usually in neat overcoats and shiny shoes. Prince William and Prince Harry often appear in matching 'yuppy'-style striped shirts and silk ties, worn under a navy blazer.

The Princess Royal's two children, Peter and Zara Phillips, are also very smartly dressed. Both look very grown up, with Peter in his tweed jacket and Zara carrying a Burberry handbag.

Zara Phillips gazes up at the grown-ups when she was spotted at the Windsor Horse Trials.

The little girl was watching the trials with her mother and was dressed appropriately in her outdoor wear.

Peter and Zara have had as normal a childhood as possible considering their relationship to the Queen. They both attend Port Regis School in Dorset and spend their weekends at their home, Gatcombe, riding their ponies and playing with the dogs.

Many of the royal children seem to be keen horse-riders. The children regularly ride their ponies in gymkhanas and belong to the Pony Club. These events provide us with lovely opportunities to photograph the young riders – if we are quick enough to spot them. It is a difficult task to recognize one face hidden by a riding hat in a sea of youngsters.

During the summer months another good opportunity to photograph royal children is at polo. Usually this will be Prince William or Prince Harry with the Princess of Wales. They regularly appear at Windsor or Cirencester to watch the Prince of Wales play. Often these polo matches can be very frustrating for us because we are put into a 'pen' to work. We can usually see the Princess playing with the boys in the far distance, and despite the wonderful long lenses these days they are still just dots on the horizon.

The children from the Kent and Gloucester families – Lady Gabriella and Lord Frederick, Prince and Princess Michael's children, and the Earl of Ulster, Lady Davina and Lady Rose, the Duke and Duchess of Gloucester's children – live with a much lower profile. We rarely see these children except on such occasions as Trooping the Colour.

The Kent children appear to be very shy, particularly Lord Freddie. He is a very beautiful child and looks very much like his mother with those wide almond-shaped eyes.

The Prince and Princess took Freddie on a special trip with them aboard the Orient Express to Venice. On arriving at Victoria Station the young Lord seemed dazed by the constant flashes and the number of photographers. He blinked from the lights and kept a very tight hold on to his mother's hand.

The Duke and Duchess of Gloucester's children have appeared on a couple of formal engagements with their parents. I remember being surprised when they turned up in London's Hyde Park at a Victorian Fayre. The children were dressed in their best clothes and were on the best behaviour. The youngest of

It is not often that we have a chance to photograph the Queen out with her grandchildren so it is a popular assignment to go to Windsor on Easter Sunday to take pictures of the Royal Family attending the family service.

Afterwards, the family go into the rectory for a short drink. Here we see the Queen leading her youngest grandson, Prince Harry, back to the Castle for lunch.

Prince William, like any other boy of seven, loves getting into mischief and playing games. In July 1989 he attended the Cartier International polo match to watch his father play.

Dressed casually in cotton shorts and T-shirt the little Prince soon became bored with looking at the horses, and, seeing his mother's handbag lying on the grass, he seized the chance for a game.

It was a good few minutes before the Princess had realised that William was using her bag as a skipping rope. The Prince, obviously aware of all the cameras pointing at him, decided it was a good opportunity to show off his wonderful skills of jumping over the bag and twirling it around his waist. The Princess just laughed at her son's antics – obviously well used to them.

the children, Lady Rose, soon became bored by the proceedings, like any small child would. She started to shuffle about and moan, and tried to escape from her parents' restraining hands. She was soon discreetly led away by her nanny.

The next time I came across Lady Rose she had grown up and was impeccably behaved on an outing with her older sister, Davina, to a pantomime in London.

To date I have not really had that many opportunities to photograph Princess Beatrice, in fact I have only seen her on three occasions; leaving hospital, her christening and departing for a summer holiday aboard *Britannia* in 1989.

For the christening I spent a long time planning how I should light the pictures. The event was to take place on a December afternoon, and I knew my biggest problem would be to get enough light for an exposure over quite a considerable distance.

At home I tried to rehearse the situation and conditions that I would be encountering, in order to

ABOVE
Two little royal holidaymakers, looking a little bored as they sit patiently on the steps of the Marivent Palace in Palma. A photocall was arranged with the Prince and Princess of Wales and their holiday hosts, King Juan Carlos and Queen Sophia of Spain, at the beginning of their Majorcan holiday in August 1989.

The boys looked as though they were counting every minute until they could speed off to the beach.

LEFT
Not even a gathering of the press corps can put Zara Phillips off her ice cream as she wanders with her nanny through the shops at the Windsor Horse Trials.

OPPOSITE
Prince Harry is seen here in his costume for his non-speaking part as a goblin in his school play back in 1987 – naturally being watched with pride by his parents.

The little Prince arrived with his classmates in costume, and we all started taking pictures. But they had masks and hats on and it was difficult to pick out young Harry, and we realised we were photographing the wrong little boy.

Suddenly someone shouted, 'He's a Goblin.' I was thrown for a second trying to remember what a goblin looked like, but luckily spotted Harry out of the corner of my eye.

ABOVE
A special treat for Prince William and Prince Harry, a ride in an open landau to watch the Trooping the Colour ceremony in 1989.

The boys sat together opposite their mother and great-grandmother as the coach proceeded down the Mall from Buckingham Palace.

OPPOSITE
Prince William seen with his two cousins Zara and Peter Phillips on the steps of Sandringham church on Christmas morning.

The children had just attended family service with the rest of the Royal Family, as is the tradition at Christmas.

The children, I am sure, could not wait to get back to the house and their presents but duty comes first even for such young royals.

do some tests. I paced out the distance on the cricket pitch outside my home and set up my ladder and flash. I had one problem, no-one to stand in as the Duchess of York, complete with a baby ... then I had an idea. I grabbed my father and persuaded him to pretend to be the Duchess. I dressed him up in a lady's red cape and a hat. I needed to see how much shadow a hat would cast. I also needed a pretend baby to see if the flash would burn out a light-coloured blanket. I rolled up a huge towel and placed it in my father's arms – this was supposed to be the baby.

We could hardly control our laughter as I took the test shots. My father looked absolutely ridiculous. Our antics became even more hysterical when a neighbour arrived home from work and peered over the fence to see what my father was up to.

After all these elaborate tests I couldn't use the lights on the day because special television lights had been erected and we all had to stick to one light source.

This was not the first time our family has had to dress up and pretend to be members of the Royal Family for test shots, and I am sure it will not be the last.

OPPOSITE
In September 1989 the Princess of Wales's brother, Viscount Althorp, married Victoria Lockwood. Great excitement surrounded this wedding, especially as Prince Harry was to be a pageboy.

A great deal of organising had gone into the arrangements for the press, and a position for forty photographers was set aside at the church's main door. Twenty-four hours before the wedding the press had already set up camp in the allotted area. We all wanted to get a front-row position as we knew in advance that Prince Harry would be wearing a large hat. This would mean not seeing his face if you were up a ladder in the third row. I was lucky and managed to grab myself a good spot.

The wedding day dawned and I felt very sorry for Viscount Althorp and his bride-to-be as the weather could not have been worse – torrential rain and very dark. I arrived at my precious spot about nine in the morning, even though the wedding was not due to take place until three. I had to guard those inches to prevent

any late-comer from sneaking into my front-row position. I was absolutely drenched as three o'clock drew near, and even my cameras looked very soggy.

As the coach carrying the bride clattered up the road, I positioned myself on a high bank surrounded by a wall with an eight-foot drop over the road. Just as the coach drew level with me I slipped and felt myself falling. I had a flash vision of landing on the roof of the coach. I do not know how, but one of my quick-thinking colleagues grabbed me and managed to pull me back. I stumbled into the press pen feeling very shaken but panicking to ensure I captured the bride alighting from the coach.

Once the wedding party had entered the church, we all had time to breathe, and then I suddenly realised that when I had stumbled I had caught my foot and had a nasty cut which was by now bleeding profusely. As usual I had no handkerchief, and my colleagues tried to persuade me to go off to a nearby first-aid point. But, knowing what devils fellow photographers can be, I did not want to lose my spot after all those hours of waiting.

Despite the rain and my little accident, all turned out well and the pictures were good, especially this one of Prince Harry looking very demure in a suit copied from a Joshua Reynolds painting that hangs in Althorp House.

LEFT
The first day at 'big' school is nerve racking enough for any child, but for a royal pupil it must be even harder with a huge crowd of press photographers and reporters waiting on the steps to capture the event.

Five-year-old Prince Harry was due to join big brother Prince William at the Notting Hill prep school Wetherby in September 1989.

We had all risen at the crack of dawn to ensure a good position opposite the school entrance. Unfortunately we were to be disappointed as Prince Harry had a virus infection and could not attend school after all. Prince William arrived alone to start the new term.

The following Monday we found ourselves repeating the exercise, up again before the dawn chorus and off to London in the hope of capturing the arrival of the new boy.

Prince Harry, completely recovered, arrived with his mother and brother William. The Princess looked on proudly as the two boys, dressed smartly in their grey and red uniforms, stood patiently. Prince Harry looked particularly pleased with his new attire, especially the school cap, and showed no signs of nerves as he eagerly followed Prince William up the steps and into the school.

❦ 9 ❦

To be a queen...past and future

The Queen Mother and the Princess of Wales are, perhaps, the two most popular royal ladies – one a Queen of the past and one a Queen of the future.

I always enjoy photographing both of them. It is interesting to stop and think just how much they have in common. Both were the youngest daughters of an Earl, both were brought up in a stately home and both have become great trend-setters in their own time.

In 1923 Lady Elizabeth Bowes Lyon married the Duke of York at Westminster Abbey when she was just twenty-two years old. The new Duchess of York was a photographer's dream, and now, over sixty-six years later, she is still a delight to photograph. Nearly always dressed in flowing dresses and ostrich-trimmed hats, the Queen Mother brings a lot of colour into our photographs.

One favourite date in a photographer's diary is the Queen Mother's birthday on 4 August. Every year we assemble in the street outside Clarence House. The Queen Mother comes down to receive flowers and cards from well-wishers. Just before lunch she appears, surrounded by members of her ever-growing family, who have been invited for the birthday lunch.

The trouble with this birthday event is that it has become so popular with the press that we have to arrive at about 6 am to secure a camera position. I am sure the Queen Mother awakes every birthday to the rattle of our stepladders as we chain them in place.

My first photograph of the Queen Mother was taken back in 1977 when she visited Polesden Lacey in Surrey.
I was rather nervous and very inexperienced at photographing the Royal Family. I shot only a few frames in colour because in those days black and white
was more popular. Considering the lack of experience and my frayed nerves I was pleased with the result, although it is very hard not to get a good picture of the Queen Mother.

The Queen Mother being greeted warmly by one of her dearest, long-standing friends, King Olav of Norway. The King and his late wife had been close to the Queen Mother since before the war, and he kissed Her Majesty's hand at Oslo airport as she arrived to join him on his eightieth birthday celebrations in May 1983.

When Lady Diana Spencer became engaged to the Prince of Wales, back in 1981, it was the Queen Mother from whom she sought guidance in preparation for her new life-style. For the five months leading up to the wedding, Lady Diana lived at Clarence House with the Queen Mother.

And now one can see how the young Princess-to-be was influenced by the Queen Mother's style, especially the pearl necklaces and feathered hats. In the ensuing years the Princess of Wales has become one of the world's most photographed women.

The Queen Mother outside her London home, Clarence House, on her eighty-eighth birthday.

The Queen Mother had received many cards and flowers and her butler is seen following behind with the biggest card of the day.

ABOVE
Certainly not looking her age, the Queen Mother smiles radiantly and waves from the balcony of her home on her eighty-ninth birthday.

Although only early in the morning, the Queen Mother is already dressed in her best clothes and hat in preparation for a family luncheon.

OPPOSITE BELOW
The Queen Mother dressed warmly against the spring air when she attended the Badminton Horse Trials.

This used to be a wonderful event for photographers, with plenty of opportunities to photograph the Royal Family casually dressed and enjoying a day at the trials. But since the Duke of Beaufort's death they have not attended.

OPPOSITE ABOVE
The Queen Mother in one of her many priceless diamond tiaras. The glittering diamonds were worn to a special banquet held in the Queen Mother's honour in Oslo, Norway.

It always amazes me that whether she is dressed in casual jeans or a formal gown she always looks marvellous. I do not know one photographer who does not enjoy photographing the Princess. And a bonus to photographers is that not only does she look so good, but she also has a great sense of humour – apparent on even the most formal of occasions. And I am sure she must need it, with the strain of being such a public person.

There are often reports about the bad relationship between the Royal Family and the press. This is true to a certain extent. I cannot blame the Royal Family for getting furious at being mis-quoted constantly and at the cameras snooping into their private lives and holidays. The Princess seems to be a very forgiving person and I have seen her behave very graciously towards reporters and photographers who may have upset her in the past.

Some days one can tell when a royal person simply does not feel like being photographed – we all have off days and I am sure royals are no different.

I remember one funny incident back in 1982 when the Princess of Wales was the subject of many

front-page stories concerning her sudden loss of weight. Rumours were rife that she had anorexia.

The Princess was due to attend a welcoming ceremony at Westminster Pier at the start of the state visit of Queen Beatrix of the Netherlands. I had what must have been the worst camera position of the day allocated to me. I was situated high up on Westminster Embankment, immediately above the jetty on which the Royal Family were standing. I had just about given up because I could not see any faces from this high angle, especially as they were wearing hats.

The Princess, perhaps now a little wary of the press, did not look up once and I despaired at the thought of trying to get that cover shot that some magazines were desperate to have that week. But my luck was to change – thanks to the misfortune of a Dutch photographer standing next to me.

The photographer had precariously balanced a lens on the ledge of the wall we were leaning over. Suddenly she knocked the lens and it tumbled into the water below. The Royal party immediately

The first of thousands of pictures I have taken of the Princess of Wales. This was my first glimpse of her as Lady Diana Spencer back in 1980.

It was well after midnight when Lady Diana emerged from the Ritz Hotel in London after dancing the night away at Princess Margaret's fiftieth birthday party. She looked freezing and rather embarrassed, huddled into her winter coat as she scuttled off past the press.

Now, nearly ten years later, it is already an historic photograph as we will never see the Princess of Wales wandering alone through the streets of London like this.

looked up to see from where the object had fallen. In those few moments I had my shot – the Princess laughed straight into my lens and I knew I had succeeded in getting a good cover picture.

It is wonderful to have two royal ladies so brightly dressed. They are years apart in age and style; the Queen Mother a leader of fashion in the 1920s in her Norman Hartnell couture garments, and the Princess of Wales in up-to-date outfits by Catherine Walker and Bruce Oldfield. Both provide us with many opportunities for good fashion shots.

The Queen Mother is never seen without a hat, except when she wears a tiara. The Princess, on the other hand, only seems to wear hats when the occasion requires it.

The Princess has wonderful legs and, of course the photographers love to capture the Princess showing them off. Some discretion is required however.

Back in the 1960s my father, then a photographer with the *Daily Express*, took a photograph of Princess Margaret climbing into a carriage. On looking at the enlargement back at the office it was clearly not a picture that the newspaper would publish as you could see the Princess's stocking tops. It was deemed 'bad taste'. I wonder if today's newspapers would have used the photograph.

In 1989 a photograph appeared of the Duchess of York's skirt being caught by the wind, revealing her underwear. I personally considered it in very poor taste. I know I would have been very upset to have seen a picture of myself like that.

I photographed the Princess of Wales alighting from a helicopter as a gust of wind was blowing her silk skirt. The hem of her petticoat was just visible, as well as her long legs, but I felt the picture was justified because it was appealing but not offensive.

The Queen Mother and the Princess of Wales, I am sure, will continue to hold much attraction for us photographers in the future and I love to reflect that maybe I will still be photographing the Princess as she approaches her eighties. But that is if I still have the energy, and survive the madness of this job!

OPPOSITE
The Princess's skirt catches the down wind of the royal helicopter as she arrives for a visit to Bath.

The skirt reveals just a little of the Princess's lace petticoat and a glimpse of her pretty royal legs.

The Princess of Wales is one of those fortunate people who looks good in almost everything – and that includes hats and tiaras. If most of us put on a tiara it would look just ridiculous but, as we can see here, on the Princess it looks stunning.

This particular tiara is an heirloom of the Spencer family and the one worn by the Princess on her wedding day. Here she is seen attending a formal banquet in Munich, 1989. Despite being almost blinded by a constant barrage of flashes, the Princess manages to keep her eyes wide open and keeps smiling on.

Lady Diana Spencer, shortly after her engagement, looks a little worried as she stands in the saddling enclosure at Sandown Racecourse in March 1981.

The future Princess had to contend with a vast press contingent this day, and it must have been a very daunting task for a shy young lady.

OPPOSITE
One of my favourite photographs of the Princess of Wales was taken in Caen, France, during the celebrations of the 900th anniversary of William the Conquerer's death.

Momentarily I failed to recognise the Princess when she arrived, as her famous blonde hair was hidden under a red-and-black bavolet-style hat.

My male colleagues were not sure it they liked the Princess wearing this style, but I certainly did. During a welcome speech, she stood looking very pensive, which gave us the chance to capture a good close-up.

OPPOSITE
A confident sophisticated Princess seen at the prestigious British Fashion Awards at London's Albert Hall in 1989.

The leader of British fashion, the Princess wears a beaded gown and matching jacket by Catherine Walker.

BELOW
Perhaps the Princess was praying that the press would go away, seen here at a polo match at Smith's Lawn, Windsor.

She was there to present the prizes. By using a long lens I was able to concentrate on capturing just the Princess. A straight-forward picture of the prize presentations would not have been so interesting to a magazine.

At last I can see the Princess's face from under her hat as she stands on Westminster Pier awaiting the arrival of Queen Beatrix in 1982.

My difficult camera position turned out to be an advantage. When the Princess looked up, the red carpet on which she was standing provided a good clear backdrop from such a high angle.

☙ 10 ❧

The Army, the Navy and the Air Force

T he Royal Family has long-standing ties with the British military forces, with some members serving a tour of duty and most holding honorary service titles.

The link with the Royal Navy is noticeably strong, probably because Prince Philip was a serving officer and currently holds the rank of Admiral of the Fleet as well as Field Marshal, Marshal of the Royal Air Force and many other honorary posts. The Prince of Wales and the Duke of York followed in their father's footsteps, and both passed out at the Royal Naval College at Dartmouth before serving as officers at sea.

Photographing members of the family during their countless visits to ships, army barracks and airbases is usually very enjoyable and nearly always produces good pictures.

As one would expect, these visits are usually very well organised, and often we are treated to some splendid hospitality, especially by the Army. The ceremonies are colourful and the uniforms very smart, in particular the vast selection worn by the family.

The Queen has been seen in only one uniform in recent years, the bright red regimental dress of the Guards. This was frequently seen being worn by Her Majesty between 1951 and 1986 at the Trooping the Colour ceremony. But due to a change of procedure, with the Queen reviewing the parade from a state landau instead of on horseback, it was decided that she would no longer wear her uniform on this ceremonial occasion. This was regretted by many because the Queen looked very elegant mounted on her famous horse, Burmese, in this splendid uniform.

The Princess Royal is Colonel-in-Chief to more than twelve regiments but we never see her in any uniform other than that denoting her position as Chief Commandant of the Women's Royal Naval Service. This uniform is extremely neat and tailored, however, and she always looks immaculately turned out during her visits to military bases. Once we saw the Princess wearing Army regulation 'denim' overalls. Although these suits are called denims, they are in fact rather like boiler suits made in heavy green cotton, and they look excellent in photographs.

It was great fun taking pictures of the Princess of Wales in a set of these denims when she visited the 13th/18th Royal Hussars at Tidworth in 1988. The Princess is their Colonel-in-Chief, and she spent the day out on the ranges on Salisbury Plain watching and taking part in exercises. It was a pleasant surprise to see her dressed in this informal manner as she stepped from a helicopter. But it would have been impossible for her to wear smart day clothes for such an event, as we found out later during a mock battle.

Princess Diana sat among camouflaged soldiers in a dugout ditch waiting to 'blow up' a bridge. Despite being only a mock battle, the atmosphere was deafening with explosions and gunfire, and there was smoke everywhere. The Princess was really enjoying all the action, but as she stepped out of the trench when all was clear, there were a few laughs from the press party standing behind her. The Princess must have been sitting on a very dusty, chalky patch of ground, and it showed. The seat of her neat green

The Duchess of York, a royal pilot, visited RAF Scampton in Lincolnshire.

After watching an exciting display by the Red Arrows, the Duchess was given the chance to fly in a small trainer aircraft. Dressed in her regulation flying suit the Duchess looked very professional as she prepared for take-off, although goodness knows how she could concentrate with all us press shuffling around the aircraft.

105

ABOVE LEFT
The Duchess of Kent smartly dressed in her dark green uniform as Controller Commandant of the Women's Royal Army Corps.

ABOVE RIGHT
The Duke of York, a serving naval officer, stands to attention and salutes his mother, the Queen, as she boards his ship, HMS Brazen, in January 1986 shortly after it berthed for a few days near London Bridge.

The Press had been keeping a close watch on the comings and goings between the ship and the shore because it was at the time of rumours of a romance involving the Prince and Sarah Ferguson.

We had hoped that Sarah would arrive to visit the Prince on board and give weight to the stories about their relationship. But after several days of watching the ship most of us had to abandon the vigil because we were due to fly off to Switzerland for a photocall

rendezvous on the ski slopes with the Prince and Princess of Wales.

And it proved to be one of those weeks for being in the wrong place at the wrong time! The very afternoon that we left, the Princess of Wales and Prince William arrived to visit HMS Brazen – accompanied by none other than Sarah Ferguson. Only a few photographers were there to get pictures, and a very depressed press corps sat in a Swiss hotel that night unable to believe we had missed it all by a few hours. Our only consolation was that Sarah's visit seemed to confirm that there was a serious romance, and that we could look forward to an engagement announcement.

The Prince of Wales, once tagged 'action man' by Fleet Street, has shown himself capable of meeting many challenges – flying, parachuting, ski-ing, shooting and riding.

He is seen here looking ready for action as co-pilot of a Hawk jet aircraft preparing for take-off during a visit to RAF Brawdy in Wales, although he is barely recognisable with his flying helmet on.

The height of the cockpit above the ground gave us photographers some trouble, but we solved this by being cheeky and pulling up a spare set of aircraft steps to climb up alongside in order to see the Prince clearly.

denims was covered with chalk. But she just giggled as she brushed off the chalk after her lady-in-waiting had informed her discreetly of the problem.

Later that day, Princess Diana arrived at another rendezvous to try her hand at driving an armoured Scorpion vehicle. To me it looked just like a tank, and I imagined that she would set off on her trial run rather jerkily like a learner driver. I was amazed as she sped off across the plains showing great driving ability.

Another Royal lady who seems to be very capable of showing the men a thing or two is the Duchess of York. As a qualified pilot of both helicopters and light aircraft, the Duchess enjoys visiting RAF bases to take the opportunity of looking over aircraft and, indeed, the chance to fly one.

In 1987 she visited the RAF Scampton base in Lincolnshire to meet the famous Red Arrows aerobatic team. After watching their spectacular air

display, the Duchess was due to fly a Bulldog trainer plane. The press, of course, lined up eagerly outside the aircraft hangar, waiting for the royal pilot who had gone off to change into regulation flying gear.

When she re-appeared, the Duchess looked very stylish in her green suit topped by her flowing red hair. We managed to take some very nice shots of her sitting in the cockpit, preparing for take-off. I can't imagine how she managed to concentrate on that task with the press corps shuffling around and clicking away with cameras.

Another keen royal flier is the Prince of Wales, and it has been possible on a number of occasions to photograph him fully clad in flying gear in the cockpit of an Air Force jet. The Prince seems to have more uniforms than any other member of the Royal Family, which is perhaps to be expected since he is heir to throne. He is Colonel-in-Chief to many regiments, naturally including the Welsh Guards, as well as the Gurkhas and the Parachute Regiment, with whom he qualified as a parachutist.

His younger brother, the Duke of York, has been the focal point of my camera on many occasions. But one event which I shall always remember was his return to England on HMS *Invincible* after serving in the Falklands War. When the great grey ship sailed back into Portsmouth Harbour in September 1982, it was one of the most emotional and patriotic events that I have ever attended, and a scene which I shall never forget.

The Princess of Wales joined the Army for the day when she visited Tidworth Barracks in Hampshire.

Much to our delight she arrived not in a formal dress or suit but wearing an all-in-one jumpsuit known as 'army denims'. This was perfect for photographs of the Princess sitting in a trench with soldiers waiting to blow up a bridge in a mock battle.

Just before lunch we were taken to Salisbury Plain to await the arrival of the Princess who was to drive an armoured vehicle. It sounded like World War III as we waited on the ranges, with tanks firing and machineguns rattling.

The Princess seemed in her element and was obviously enjoying her day with the Army immensely. The prospect of the Princess driving an armoured vehicle promised to be a good photograph – something out of the ordinary. And once the royal driver had squeezed herself into the small hatch at the top of the heavy vehicle, to our amazement she proceeded to drive off very expertly across the plains.

A 'regimental' touch to her choice of dress made the Princess of Wales look the part for photographers when she reviewed young officers on parade at the Sandhurst Military Academy in a cream braided suit and high hat.

The Queen went aboard as soon as the ship docked to welcome everyone home, and shortly afterwards Prince Andrew came ashore in a highly jubilant mood. It was one of those occasions guaranteed to make photographers scream with frustration if their film runs out just at the vital moment. The Prince was jumping up and down on the quayside, waving a rose in the air. Suddenly he put it into his mouth in the style of a Flamenco dancer. My film had come to the last frame a second or two earlier, and by the time I had reloaded he had moved off. Naturally I was deeply disappointed at missing such a shot, but these things happen to all of us quite regularly.

A highlight of the Duke and Duchess of York's official tour of California was a 5½-hour visit to the nuclear-powered aircraft carrier USS Nimitz. The crew of the Nimitz, sailing off the San Diego coastline, provided a spectacular display for the royal guests.

The Duke of York was also given the chance of a 160-mph slingshot take-off from the ship aboard a Viking jet.

The Duchess, who was grounded because of her pregnancy, laughed and joked with the captain of the ship as they awaited the departure of the jet carrying the Duke. Everyone in the take-off area, including the Duchess, had to dress in protective clothing and headgear.

Helicopter pilot Prince Andrew showed his happiness to be back at his home base at Culdrose in Cornwall only twenty-four hours after coming ashore from HMS Invincible, the ship on which he served for six months during the Falklands War.

A celebration was held at the side of the runway to welcome home members of 820 Sea King Squadron, at which the young Prince joined his flying friends and their families for a glass of champagne while relating tales of their adventures.

I felt a little happier a day or so later when I managed to take some very relaxed pictures of the Prince when he returned to his home base at Culdrose in Cornwall. Luckily a colleague and I had been talking to people in the crowd at Portsmouth and we were told that Prince Andrew would be attending a special celebration at Culdrose. We kept this valuable information to ourselves, and set off for Cornwall.

The young Prince arrived as promised in his helicopter, and the celebrations began at the side of the runway on landing. We took some very happy pictures of a returning royal hero.

Military passing-out parades are usually very colourful, full of tradition and all the ingredients for a good picture. The Sandhurst passing-put parade is one of the best, with various members of the Royal Family representing the Queen at the review.

In 1986, the Princess of Wales was present there, and her choice of dress became the focus of comment, as well as our cameras. The Princess does

The Queen sits side-saddle on her famous mount, Burmese, during the Trooping the Colour ceremony on London's Horseguards Parade.

The ability of a woman of her age to sit in this position for more than one hour, looking immaculate throughout in her brillant red regimental uniform, demands everyone's admiration.

Regrettably, in recent years the Queen has decided to review the parade from an open landau – a sensible switch, even if not so photogenic.

The Princess of Wales represented the Queen at the passing-out parade of officer cadets at the Britannia Royal Naval College in Dartmouth in 1989.

While Princess Diana does not have a naval uniform by any courtesy rank, her choice of dress was regarded as perfect – with a nautical-style tricorn hat matching a bright red-and-white coat-dress. As she inspected the parade, her colourful outfit stood out clearly amidst the dark blue uniforms of the cadets.

The Prince of Wales, dressed smartly in his tropical white uniform as a Naval Commander during a visit to the Commonwealth cemetery on the outskirts of Jakarta, Indonesia.

The Prince was promoted to the rank of Commander on his fortieth birthday in 1988.

The Princess Royal on parade as the Chief Commandant of the Womens Royal Naval Service. The royal visitor was inspecting the ranks during a visit to HMS Royal Arthur in Hampshire.

The uniform of dark-navy blue worn under the regulation coat looked extremely smart on the Princess.

not have an Army uniform, and she chose for the event a two-piece suit in a military style with gold braiding similar to that of a Royal Hussars uniform. Personally I liked her choice and I thought it blended well with this military occasion. It showed her sense of fun, which was evident again in her choice of clothes for the passing-out parade of officers at the Royal Naval College at Dartmouth in 1989. For this the Princess wore a red-and-white dress with a large tricorn hat.

The Duchess of Kent looks extremely elegant in her uniform as Controller Commandant of the Women's Royal Army Corps, although frequently she wears civilian dress for her visits.

For photographers like myself with no military background or knowledge, it can be very confusing, trying to identify all the different uniforms for our captions. But I would not miss these events because they are highly dramatic, very enjoyable and wonderful opportunities for good photographs.

Days of relaxation

The Princess of Wales enjoys an afternoon off at Smith's Lawn, Windsor, while her husband plays polo.

The Prince's team, 'Windsor Park', had just won their match and here the royal player shares his victory with a friend and fellow player.

D ays of relaxation are few and far between for us photographers, especially during the summer months. Members of the Royal Family spend their weekends in a variety of ways, and this means a lot of work for us.

Polo spoils my summers. Just as I am immersed in mowing my lawn or cutting the roses I suddenly remember it is time to wash up and rush off to polo at Windsor or Cirencester. The Prince of Wales is a very keen polo player, as was his father in his younger days. During the polo season the Prince may play polo up to four times a week if his official duties permit. It may be an exciting game to play but I find it very boring to watch. However, I cannot miss these matches as they produce good informal photographs of the Prince and other members of the family who may turn out to watch.

As spectators, members of the Royal Family are invariably casually dressed. The Princess of Wales may appear in jeans and a baseball cap, and that is the picture we do not get if we miss this type of event.

Horse shows are also popular with the Royal Family. A number are held in the Queen's grounds at Windsor, the most important being the Royal Windsor Horse Show. The Queen excitedly appears with her camera to watch and record Prince Philip competing in the driving Grand Prix. These events provide good entertainment for the royals, and often the Queen has a number of house guests who enjoy watching the events from the Royal Box or the back of the Queen's Range Rover.

A very popular way to relax for the Royal Family is to go for a quiet country hack. Being a keen family of horse riders the royal stables at Windsor, Sandringham and Balmoral are always busy, and a lot of organising goes in to moving their favourite horses and ponies around the country.

During the winter months some of the Royal Family like to take a ski-ing holiday on the slopes of

During the summer months the Queen spends many of her weekends at Windsor Castle. Often on a Sunday afternoon Her Majesty likes to drive to Smith's Lawn in Windsor Great Park to watch Prince Charles play polo. On these occasions she often dresses as casually as possible. Usually a silk headscarf keeps the Royal locks in place without the formality of wearing a hat.

Here we see the Queen on one such occasion when she presented the winning polo team with rosettes. One of the Queen's best assets is her wonderful smile – Prince Charles must have been among the prize winners since the Queen looked extremely happy.

One usually thinks of the Duke of Edinburgh as having a rather serious nature but occasionally one has a chance to capture his sense of humour.

On this particular day the Duke was attending a charity event, the 'Ascot Spectacular', with Prince Edward at Ascot racecourse.

During the afternoon the royal visitors sat in the stands to watch a parachute display. Something obviously caught the Duke's eye as he sat roaring with laughter and clapping along with the crowd.

As I had my back to whatever was happening, I am unable to unravel the mystery of what kept the Duke so amused.

You could easily walk past the Queen and not notice her as she stands among the crowd at the Royal Windsor Horse Show.

Dressed very casually in a coat and headscarf the Queen ventures out with her camera to record Prince Philip's carriage as it speeds around the cross-country course.

Europe. Even though there is a fair amount of press attention on these holidays the family can still enjoy some peaceful mountain air.

The keenest skiers seem to be the Prince and Princess of Wales and the Duchess of York. It is hoped that Prince William will soon join his parents on the slopes – we cannot wait to take pictures of the little royal skier.

The Princess Royal is also a proficient skier, as are her children. They often quietly slip off for a week in Switzerland.

The Duchess of Kent does not ski but still accompanies her husband and family on their holiday for the fresh air.

The Duke and Duchess of Gloucester are keen skiers, and accompanied the Prince of Wales on a number of ski-ing holidays before his engagement to Lady Diana.

A typical day of royal relaxation certainly never seems to include a lazy afternoon of putting up one's feet and having a snooze. Whether it is riding, fishing, shooting, sailing or walking, they never seem to sit still.

It keeps us press photographers exhausted . . .

It is not very often that we see the Queen wearing trousers; in fact I can only remember seeing her on one occasion other than here with slacks on. The Queen, having just been for a quiet country ride through her estate at Windsor, pops down to the Royal Windsor Horse Show to watch Prince Philip competing.

The previous occasion I had seen the Queen dressed in trousers was during a visit to a game reserve in Zambia when she wore a loose blouse and straight brown trousers.

Another keen horsewoman in the Royal Family is Princess Michael of Kent. The Princess hunts regularly with her husband and occasionally she competes in small one-day events.

The Princess is photographed here taking part in the Amberley horse trials. During a break the Princess posed briefly for us with her horse.

❧ 12 ❧

Behind the camera

This is the sight that greets the Prince and Princess of Wales as they ski down the slopes towards the waiting hordes of press.

A location has been agreed and members of the press are seen here waiting for the Prince and Princess to arrive to begin a short photocall. Photographers from all over Europe are here in large numbers. The tranquility of the mountain is broken, and it must present a rather bizarre scene to unsuspecting fellow skiers who have not heard what is going on.

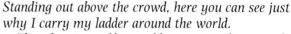

If you look very carefully you can just spot a small part of the future Duchess of York's red hair in the crowd of press.

This was the scene as Sarah Ferguson arrived at her London office during the royal romance rumours. In these situations you are extremely lucky to get a clear shot, especially as you spend your time running backwards.

As you can see, I am in the wrong spot behind the Duchess, swallowed up in the crowd and unable to get a shot.

Standing out above the crowd, here you can see just why I carry my ladder around the world.

The advantage of being able to tower above people's heads in these situations makes it worthwhile. I can see clearly and not have to jostle with everyone – except when someone decides to try and climb up on the ladder, too.

A London street is turned into chaos for a few days. The press corps gathers in preparation for the departure of the Duchess of York with her new-born daughter, Princess Beatrice, from the Portland Hospital in London's West End.

The press has been penned into an area by the police, and cordoned off with cones. What a daunting sight for the Duchess and her baby as they step into the daylight!

A glamorous job? You must be joking. Here you can see me resembling a drowned rat as I wait for the Princess of Wales to arrive for an official engagement one evening in Swansea, Wales.

At this point you can see I have given up trying to keep myself or my camera dry as the rain continues to pour down. I end up getting no pictures at all after such a long drive and a tedious wait.

*My own personal bodyguards – no such luck, although
it would come in extremely handy to keep my colleagues
in control during a rush for a prized position in the press
pen.*

*Here, for a change, I take a few minutes' break during
the Queen's visit to Jordan for a few happy snaps of my
own.*